FREDDIE FLINTOFF

RIGHT, SAID FRED

BLINK
bringing you closer

First published in the UK by Blink Publishing
an imprint of Bonnier Books UK
The Plaza
535 Kings Road, London, SW10 0SZ
Owned by Bonnier Books
Sveavägen 56, Stockholm, Sweden

facebook.com/blinkpublishing
twitter.com/blinkpublishing

Hardback: 978-1-788-701-98-3
Signed: 978-1-788-703-94-9
Trade Paperback: 978-1-788-703-07-9
Paperback: 978-1-788-704-14-4
Ebook: 978-1-788-703-06-2
Audiobook: 978-1-788-704-06-9

A CIP catalogue of this book is available from the British Library.

Designed and set by seagulls.net
Printed and bound by Clays Ltd, Elcograf S.p.A

1 3 5 7 9 10 8 6 4 2

Blink Publishing is an imprint of Bonnier Books UK
www.bonnierbooks.co.uk

Andrew 'Freddie' Flintoff (MBE) is a bestselling author, broadcaster and former England international cricketer. He lives with his wife, Rachael, and their four children.

Freddie won BBC Sports Personality of the Year in 2005. Following his retirement from sport, he joined the panel of BAFTA-winning *A League of Their Own* and now is a presenter on BBC's ever-popular and award-winning *Top Gear*. He has presented documentaries and interviewed some of the world's most famous figures. He has written for newspapers, fronted his own radio show and had a hugely successful podcast, Flintoff, Savage and the Ping Pong Guy.

CONTENTS

CHAPTER ONE

CAR COMPETITION

When I heard that Jeremy Clarkson had been sacked from *Top Gear* for punching an Irishman, I got straight on the phone to my agents and said, 'I want to do that job.' They replied, 'Yeah, I can see it actually.' And I replied, 'Go on then, see what you can do ...' Up until then, I'd kind of stumbled into everything. And out of all the jobs in TV, presenting *Top Gear* was the one I really wanted to do. That and presenting *Question Time*, but even I had to admit that unless every political journalist in the country was simultaneously wiped out in some freak accident, that was unlikely to happen.

Every idea I'd ever come up with, my agents Richard and Katie had managed to get me in front of the right people. But I'm glad they weren't able to work a miracle in 2015. Not that I was really in a position to take the job anyway, but taking over from Clarkson, James May and Richard Hammond would have been a poisoned chalice. Look what happened to Chris Evans when he started presenting the show – he got destroyed by the public and the media. I wasn't surprised. Not that I've got anything against Chris, but Clarkson had made that show his own. I'm not sure I'd want to be mates with him – or if you're even allowed to like him – but he was brilliant on *Top Gear*. How could he not have been? He made it one of the biggest shows in the world.

Three years later, I'd just finished filming an episode of *A League of Their Own*, which involved crawling through a muddy assault course in the studio, when my agent Richard wandered over with a big smile on his face and said, 'I've got some good news. But you're going to have to sit down.' I did as I was told and Richard said, '*Top Gear* have been on the phone and they want you to do a screen test next week, if you're up for it.' I didn't get too excited, because a screen test is just a trial, not a job offer. But I was bang up for it.

The opportunity had come at exactly the right time. I'd been thinking a lot about my TV career and whether I should do something else instead. I was still loving being on *A*

League of Their Own, because I'd been doing it for eight years and grown so close to my fellow panellists, especially Jamie Redknapp and Romesh Ranganathan. But otherwise I was thinking about packing all the other TV stuff in. I didn't want to do anything I wasn't really interested in, so I was thinking about carrying on with *A League of Their Own*, doing some cricket commentary or presenting, and spending the rest of my time pottering. I enjoy being on TV and work hard at it, but it was never my dream and doesn't give me the same buzz as being a cricketer. Playing cricket for Lancashire and England was all I'd ever wanted to do. So I knew that walking away from TV work wouldn't be the same emotional wrench as retiring from cricket.

On a more basic level, I just loved cars. The car has got to be one of the greatest and most important inventions in history, right up there with the printing press, the light bulb and penicillin. The car is one of the few inventions that fundamentally changed the way humans lived, literally broadened people's horizons. Nowadays, people will try to make you feel guilty about owning a car, unless it's electric.

First, there isn't an electric car I like. Second, we don't have the infrastructure, in terms of enough charging points. Third, they're not actually that good for the environment. Yes, they produce less pollution, but making the batteries requires the mining of rare metals and a lot of extra energy. I'll need to have driven quite a lot of miles in my petrol car before it has the same environmental impact as a brand-new electric car. And because I change my cars quite a lot, I'm probably doing less damage to the environment than someone who drives an electric car. I'm not some knee-jerk reactionary who is against electric cars on principle, I'd actually like to get one eventually. But only when the cars get better, the infrastructure improves and it can be proved beyond doubt that driving one is better for the planet.

But whether you're into electric cars or petrol, gears or automatics, cars are such a big part of our everyday life that I struggle with people who say they're not into cars. They're lying. If you own a car and you drive a car, then you're into cars. You might not know anything about cars, but you're into them, whether you think you are or you don't. And I really can't get my head around people who don't drive. I can't even imagine it. When I was a kid, I couldn't wait to be 17 so that I could get behind a wheel. It meant freedom, being able to go wherever I wanted and do whatever I wanted. The reason I failed my test the first two times was because it was so important to me. The first time I failed on a dangerous (I thought there was more than enough room on the roundabout to get home, he disagreed). The second time I got a minor fault. As soon as I'd done it, I knew I'd failed. So I thought, 'I'm going to give him the ride of his life ...' The third time I knew the bloke, which was nice. He played cricket for Morecambe and I used to play against him, so we talked about old times for 20 minutes before he said, 'You better do one of those emergency stops. If you want.' That was pretty much that, he passed me.

My first car was a black Fiat Uno, which I rented for a few months after passing my test (at the third attempt). Driving it, I looked like one of the Ant Hill Mob from *Wacky Races*, because I could almost stick my arms out of the windows and pick it up. When you're a cricketer, you're always trying to get a car for free. Even to this day, I'm always trying to get free cars, it's just ingrained in me. My missus had a Kia Sorento for a while, because I got it for free. Don't get me wrong, it was a lovely car. But after a while she started asking questions, because it was usually parked next to my Ferrari. Back when I started playing, some of the older players had their names on the side of their cars: 'Neil Fairbrother – sponsored by Lookers'. I didn't want that, but Lancashire had a deal with Rover whereby I could rent one of their cars for 1 per cent of its value a month, plus about 30 quid for insurance. That worked out at about 150 quid a month. It's not as if they were going to let me have a 220 Turbo, so my first Rover was a 216 Coupé. I didn't drink at the time, so used to ferry my mates around on nights out. And every night without fail I'd get stopped by the police, because driving that car in Preston was the equivalent of driving a McLaren in Chelsea. I upgraded to a 216 cabriolet in blue, but there was obviously a mix-up, because when it arrived it was purple. So when I got a pay rise, I upgraded to a 620ti, which wasn't quite the stuff of Alan Partridge's dreams (I believe he drove a Rover 825), but not far off. Alas, someone went into the back of it when I was on my way to a game in Cheadle. On the bright side, I got a grand for the whiplash, taped the boot closed and carried on.

The first car I bought was a Porsche Boxster on tick when I was 21 (which came in handy on *Top Gear*, because one of the episodes involved us driving around Ethiopia in our first cars – Paddy had an Escort 1.6 and Chris had a Mini). I was on tour in Pakistan at the time and obviously feeling a bit bored and sorry for myself. When it turned up, it wasn't quite the colour I thought it was going to be. I knew it was going to be blue, but it was a bit brighter than advertised. But I loved that car, until one night I was driving down a country lane in Hale. It was quite icy, so I was taking plenty of care, creeping around these corners at 10 mph, when this B-registration Metro came hurtling towards me. I slammed on the brakes, but this Metro couldn't stop and hit me front on. It hadn't been going very fast – 5 mph at most – but the whole of my front end fell off. This Metro didn't have a scratch on it and its driver refused liability. So after that, the gloves came off.

My next car was a BMW M5, which came third-hand via the golfers Lee Westwood and Darren Clarke, who were part of the same management company. That car was a dream, unlike the Overfinch Range Rover I made the mistake of buying. I drove over a pothole and two wheels cracked, and when I drove through a big puddle (I promise it was nothing more than that), the undertray fell off.

When I took it back to the garage the bloke said, 'What have you been doing?'

'I drove through a puddle ...'

I picked the car up three days later, drove through the same puddle on the way home (at nothing more than 30 mph) and the undertray fell off again, so I gave it back. When it comes to cars, appearance can be deceptive.

My Ford F-150 Harley Davidson pickup was a beautiful thing to look at – to drive, not so much. In a straight line it was a scream, but around corners the back end was everywhere, unless you had a tonne of bricks in the back. Which, funnily enough, I never did. I was driving to a mate's house one day, went round a bend (not that fast, I should add) and the back end came out. When I tried correcting it, it went the other way and ploughed through a fence. I ended up in a field with half a bush in my car, because I had the windows down. When I tried to start it again, it was knackered. I got out, this bloke came over to see if I was all right and we had started having a bit of a laugh. Bad timing. Right on cue, the farmer's wife turned up with some field hands and started shouting at me about the fact I could have killed her horses. I tried to defuse the situation with a bit of humour – 'Oh, I did notice some horses, but they must have scarpered when they saw me coming through the fence' – but that didn't go down too well either and everyone started shouting at me even louder. So I walked the rest of the way to my mate's house and a few hours later flew over the wreck in his helicopter, on the way to the races. I did eventually get the car towed out, but never drove it again.

There came a time when England cricketers stopped driving Rovers with their name on the side and started driving significantly more extravagant vehicles, but not many could afford anything ridiculous. I recall Kevin Pietersen driving a Ferrari before the 2009 Ashes series, but he was paying an extortionate amount of money and only had it for a few weeks. I used to get a deal from Volkswagen, and it was only really when I stopped playing cricket that I started wasting money on cars. When I was asked to try out for *Top Gear*, my daily drive was a ten-year-old black Porsche 997 Turbo, which was just about everything I wanted in a car. Plus, I had a Mercedes GLS350d for family stuff, a Ferrari 612 Scaglietti and a Lamborghini Murcielago. That car was a work of art and just beautiful to look at, but I felt like a knobhead driving it. It had carbon bucket seats that you couldn't put back, I couldn't use the indicator going left because my knee was in the way and after driving it for more than half an hour I was sore. In the end, I had to get rid of it. That was a shameful story in itself. This fella came round to pick it up, because he was taking it to a garage in Preston to sell it for me, and my drive was covered in cars. I have an irrational hatred of other people's cars being on my drive, it just makes me very angry. So I probably backed the Lambo out of my garage a bit sharpish and went straight into my Rolls-Royce Phantom. At that point, my anger curdled into disappointment at what I'd become. I stormed into the house and started shouting about selling everything – the Lambo, the Rolls, the Ferrari, the Porsche, the lot!

I'd wanted a Rolls-Royce for years and particularly loved the look of the Phantom Drophead. The only thing that stopped me from buying one was the prospect of looking like a dick. But when I drove one, I had to have it. Looking back, I don't know whether that was a moment of weakness or strength. It's an amazing car but there are still times when I think, 'I'm driving a Rolls. Does this make me a complete bellend?' There are certain places I'll take it and certain places I won't. I'd think twice about taking it back to Preston and when I take it to the gym, it either looks like I've stolen it or I'm cleaning it for someone more sophisticated than me. For a while, I told myself I was driving it ironically. But I got that out of my system. It's a beautiful car, a work of art as much as anything, and I just love looking at it and driving it.

I don't like spending lots of money on things, apart from cars. They're my only real extravagance and I've learned not to feel apologetic about owning them. I'm not passionate about many other things and don't have many other hobbies, and it's not as if I'm driving around with the windows down, shouting, 'I'm here in my Rolls! Look at me! Look at me!' And because

I spend a lot of time in my cars, I want cars that I really like. Unlike other things, the joy of owning, looking at and driving a beautiful car never really wears off, at least not for me.

But I digress (cars have that effect on me). The screen test was at some army place in Nottingham, which was handy, because the boys were playing in a cricket tournament nearby and I could slip off for the day. I'd be lying if I said I wasn't a little bit nervous. It wasn't like when I auditioned for the musical *Fat Friends*, when I was thinking, 'It will be nice if I get this, but no problems if not.' I really wanted the gig, it was what I really wanted to do, so the competitive juices were flowing. They'd sent me a script, but I only scanned it. That wasn't me being cocky, I just didn't see myself as a presenter. If they'd wanted a presenter, they could have found loads who were better than me at learning lines and reading an autocue. The best chance I had of landing the job was simply by being me.

I did learn a few things about the car I was asked to drive, a Dacia Duster, and I very quickly forgot that the cameras were rolling. I was paired with Chris Harris, who can review a car better than anyone. After we'd spent a couple of hours dicking about, I thought I'd done okay, because the people in charge started talking about concrete things like filming dates. They told me that they were making the decision the following week, and I was desperate to get the gig, but when I didn't hear anything then, or the week after, or the week after that, I thought they'd plumped for someone else. Then one day, about six weeks after my screen test, I was in the back of Rachael's car, travelling through Altrincham with the kids, and Richard called. He said, 'Are you on your own?'

'No. I'm in the car. But I'll get Rachael to stop somewhere.'

Rachael pulled over, I got out and Richard said, 'You've got the job.'

Not many things excite me, but this did. The only thing I can compare it to is getting that phone call saying I'd been selected for England. It wasn't as big, because playing for England was a childhood dream and winning my first England cap came out of the blue, but it was a similar feeling. And, in a weird way, it made me happier, maybe because I'd started to think I'd never do anything again that really thrilled me. I loved cars and I loved travelling, so it was another dream job. I couldn't get my head around it for weeks. I had no idea why they picked me, and I tried not to think about it. Why did it matter?

Things started snowballing from there, although I had to keep the whole thing a big secret, like I'd become a Freemason. And when my eldest son got all excited about me working with Joey from *Friends*, I had to explain to him that the reason I'd been offered the job was because Joey had left. I kept looking online, to see if anything had leaked. Occasionally, I'd see quotes from someone else, saying they were in the frame, and I'd say, 'Sorry, it's not you mate.' Then, a couple of weeks after accepting the job, I discovered that my co-presenter would be Paddy McGuinness. We didn't know each other that well but the idea of two Lancashire lads – me from Preston and Paddy from Bolton – presenting *Top Gear* made me happy. And when me, Paddy and Chris spent a day filming together, doing promotional photos, messing about and getting to know each other, I started thinking, 'You know what? We might just be all right here ...'

I knew there would be some negativity surrounding the new presenting line-up. *Top Gear* is meant to be a show about the fun that can be had driving cars, but some people take it far more seriously than that. Fans talk about it almost as if it's sacred, and the way journalists write about it, you'd think it was the *News at Ten*. Clarkson, May and Hammond had built it into this global brand that had obviously become very important to the BBC, and when Clarkson got sacked and the others left as well, people lost their shit. But I had to ignore all of that, otherwise I'd have been overcome by fear and unable to do it. It helped that I'd done serious stuff, including documentaries on mental health and eating disorders, useful programmes that might actually help people. So I was able to think, 'You know what? *Top Gear* is the biggest and best TV job you'll ever have. That on its own is enough to keep you on your toes. You might get found out, but what's the worst that can happen? You're not saving lives or anything, you're just presenting a programme about cars. Some people will watch it, some won't. It's just a bit of TV, that's all it is.'

I didn't think about trying to compete with Clarkson, May and Hammond and being bigger and better. I was the 591st man to play Tests for England, which meant there were 590 men that came before me (including a May and a Hammond, both of them greats). I was always thankful for them paving the way, and that's how I thought about Clarkson, May and Hammond. They had made *Top Gear* their own and were brilliant on it. So I understood why Clarkson made a few barbed comments about *Top Gear* after leaving. I'd have even understood if he'd come out and admitted he wanted it to go tits up. Clarkson said that when he was sacked from the show, it was like someone taking his baby away, and I can understand that. When I retired from cricket, I wasn't ready to leave the stage either. And when someone else took my job, it was difficult. For Clarkson, it was Chris Evans, Matt LeBlanc and then me and Paddy. For me, it was Ben Stokes. Things move on so fast and you're quickly forgotten. Good job, too, because if you're not quickly forgotten, things can't be going right in your absence. I don't resent Ben Stokes, and I don't want him to fail (although I might resent him and want him to fail if he retired from cricket and nicked my job on *Top Gear*). But there would be something wrong with me if I didn't think, 'I'd love to still be doing what he's doing.'

When I performed *Fat Friends*, we were only allowed to pin good reviews on the noticeboard. But I pinned one up that absolutely hammered me, I was honestly fine about it, I just did it as a joke. I'd like to think I was as blasé about the prospect of bad reviews for *Top Gear*, but if you've got every newspaper in the country hammering you, rather than the odd critic from the Lancashire press, I'm sure it takes its toll. But I'd taken plenty of flak as a cricketer. And, when it comes to TV, the public ultimately decides what someone can and can't do. When I say 'the public', I don't mean people ranting and raving and being abusive on social media, I mean people voting with their remote controls. If they switch off, the show goes under and/or I get canned. If they don't, the show carries on and I can carry on presenting it.

When it came to starting filming, I was almost as excited as I'd been during my cricket career. I hadn't had that feeling for a long time. When that music came on and I was stood there in the middle with Paddy and Chris, I couldn't help thinking how bizarrely my life had turned out. I enjoyed doing the bits and pieces in the studio, but that world always feels a bit unnatural to me. I've never been a slave to the autocue, and they let me interpret things in my own way (because if I'm reading, you *really* know that I'm reading), but I prefer being out and about than doing links or presenting. I find it far easier reacting to things that naturally happen, which I suppose you would describe as being a bit loose and playing a slightly exaggerated version of yourself.

Before *Top Gear*, the TV jobs I'd loved most were those that gave me the opportunity to travel and all the life experiences that come with that. *Top Gear* was the same, in that we became totally immersed in wherever we ended up. In somewhere like Ethiopia, you stay where you can. It might be a nice lodge, but it might be little more than a hut. That's fine with me, because I don't really want to be staying in the Four Seasons anyway. I was blown away by Ethiopia, not least because even all these years later, I still associated it with its famine in the 1980s. But it was green and lush and absolutely beautiful.

Peru was incredible, one of the best places I'd ever been, with the loveliest, most welcoming people. Apparently, the Incas built their roads hundreds of years ago and they were so far ahead of their time, I couldn't help thinking that aliens were somehow involved. Like the pyramids in Egypt, I just don't see how it was possible otherwise. Driving through Peru was just incredible – Chris in his Dart, me in my VW campervan, which I've always loved but had never had the chance to drive. Travelling with Paddy was brilliant, because he's so enthusiastic about everything. By his own admission, he wasn't very well travelled before he did *Top Gear*, so he was like someone who had opened his eyes for the very first time. And that kind of child-like curiosity is infectious.

I don't think I could have done the job a few years earlier, because I didn't listen too much when I was playing cricket. I rated myself as a driver, but I'm pretty sure every bloke does. And you've got to listen hard when someone is teaching you how to drive a car at 150 mph, otherwise things can go wrong. And even when you do listen, things can still go wrong. Which they did. The second crash happened in Mansfield, when I was racing Paddy and Chris around the city centre, misjudged a bend and ploughed my retro pickup truck straight into a market stall. Luckily, the market stall was empty. The first was when I rolled a hearse in Wales. I blame Chris for that one. I was trying to muscle this hearse around a corner, he was egging me on and I hit a bump. Having lost control of the wheel for a second I thought, 'We're going to be all right, it's going to come back', before the hearse started to go over and everything seemed to slow down. I'd rolled a car and it felt the same, so when we were upside down I thought, 'Actually, we'll be all right.' It was only when I heard Chris shouting to Paddy in the back, and not getting a reply, that I started panicking. It's one thing hurting yourself, but you don't want to hurt anyone else. Luckily, Paddy wasn't dead, he was just in a state of shock.

Then there was the time I crashed a three-wheeled cycle-car during a drag race at Elvington Airfield. I was lying on my front, hurtling along at 124 mph (which, to be fair to the vehicle's owner, was 4 mph faster than he told me it could go) when I overshot the runaway and spun off. People told me there was a huge bang before I disappeared in a cloud of dust. Elvington was where Richard Hammond almost killed himself while filming for *Top Gear* a few years back, so Paddy, Chris and the crew were obviously quite concerned. But after being checked over by the medics, I was back on my feet and back at it. The media made it sound as if I'd almost died, but when the footage was broadcast, it looked more ridiculous than dangerous. And it took my kids two days to find out how I was: 'Mum said you had a bit of an accident?'

Me and Paddy were half-decent drivers (and Paddy says he likes to tinker under the bonnet, although I haven't seen any evidence of that yet), but when we saw what Chris could do behind a wheel, we realised we were nowhere near. I like how they look, I like driving them, I know a fast car from a slow car, and I can probably do what most men can do: fill them up with petrol, check the oil, change a tyre. But that's about it. I'm not a mechanic or a racing driver, and I'm not trying to be anything I'm not. And I've never met anyone who knows as much about cars as Chris, which is why I ask him questions all the time. It's like being a kid in a cricket team, soaking up knowledge from the senior player. When Chris speaks, we listen, even if we don't know what he's talking about, which is a lot of the time. It's also why Chris does most of the 'proper' driving. He can do pieces to camera while driving at 200 mph in a Ferrari 488 – sideways. He'll be talking as if he's tootling down to the supermarket: 'What do I need to get again? Bread and milk?' I didn't want any of my driving to be faked, so when you see me flying around a track, that's actually me – they don't do close-ups of my face and cut to long shots of someone else behind the wheel. If Chris is driving something, that probably means neither me nor Paddy could do it.

My driving is getting better, which means I'm getting to do more and more things. I love driving a car very fast around a track, but it's the off-road driving I enjoy most. Me and Chris competed in the Formula Offroad in Iceland, which involves driving 1600 horsepower buggies up the sides of cliffs. We also competed in the Baja 1000 in Mexico, but I didn't get the chance to drive because the car fell apart while Chris was doing the first leg. But I can't see myself driving in any kind of professional capacity any time soon.

There are different levels of competition and I could probably get into some of them. But first, I don't really have the time. And second, I couldn't be doing with all the faffing about. If you could just turn up to the track, jump in the car and drive, that would be brilliant. But you've got to test them and go through all the mechanics and the rest, which would just bore me. Plus, my competitive spirit has nearly disappeared. Whether it's *Top Gear* or *A League of Their Own*, I do a lot of competitive stuff, but I'm not bothered about winning any more. I know where desperately wanting to win takes me, because that's how I used to live my life. And it's not a fun place. When you're a sportsperson, winning takes on a whole different meaning. It's literally your job to win. But needing to win all the time is exhausting. I no longer want to be like that, because if all your energy is focused on winning, you miss out on other stuff – like enjoying yourself, which is what I'm supposed to be doing now. In my new career, I'm not judged on winning or losing. Driving around a dirt track while someone is squirting cattle lubricant in your face isn't exactly the Ashes. That's not to say I don't still have to work on it. There was one segment in the last series of *Top Gear* that involved us playing the equivalent of musical chairs with cars. I was driving and I completely wiped Chris out.

I wasn't particularly proud of myself. For that split second, the competitive juices started surging through my veins and I had to have that parking spot.

I've driven an Austin Allegro through Borneo and an old Porsche Boxster through Ethiopia, as well as a £250,000 car around a track, which is impossible not to love. I did sometimes think, 'This is madness', but the only time I say no to anything is if I think it's a shit idea, not because it might be dangerous. So when they said they wanted me to do a bungee jump in Switzerland, off a 400-ft dam in a convertible Metro, I immediately said yes.

I'd done bungee jumps before, including off a dam for *A League of Their Own*. And while I realised that there were a few more moving parts involved doing a bungee jump in a car, I wasn't too bothered. It just seemed like a fun way to spend an afternoon, and I was sure they'd filled in all the relevant health and safety forms. The stunt was dressed up as an experiment, to prove that a nineties' Rover can accelerate faster than an Ariel Atom, which can go from 0–60 mph in just over two seconds. In truth, it was a bit of theatre designed to scare the shit out of me. Because everything had to look perfect for TV and they had to set up lots of different camera shots, I was sitting in that car for an hour and a half. After about five minutes, I started to feel quite comfortable. It was a case of, 'Right, lads, I'm ready when you are, drop me whenever you want.' But after about half an hour, lots of things started going through my mind. When you're doing a normal bungee jump, you've got a rope around your feet, so you know you're attached to something. But in a car, you can't feel anything. You're just suspended in mid-air. So I started thinking, 'This car is just attached to a crane. What if the crane isn't properly attached to something and topples over? And that crane driver didn't look too confident. I hope these ropes are going to kick in ... Why am I doing this?' It was utterly terrifying. And when they finally dropped me, it was truly horrific.

Having done that bungee jump, I do wonder what they're going to come up with next. What I do know is that they've already got their most depraved minds on it.

It doesn't matter what it is – business, politics, acting, sport or TV – once you start thinking you've cracked it and are doing well, that's when it will all come crashing down. But our first series of *Top Gear* was a great start. The relationships between the three presenters got tighter episode after episode and it gave us a great platform to build on. The humour wasn't the same as in the Clarkson era, because it couldn't be. The world has changed and things that used to be acceptable aren't any more. We just don't come close to the line that shouldn't be crossed. It's more about having a laugh and rooting for each other. Then, in the second series, we were able to push the boundaries a bit more and do even more audacious things. The ratings for the first two series were so good that they're moving the third series from BBC2 to BBC1, for the first time in its modern history. People wanted their *Top Gear* back, and I'm so pleased we were able to give it to them. One thing's for sure, *Top Gear* fans have been more positive than cricket fans were when I was playing.

Personally, I always just tried to be myself, which seems to have worked. I've also got more confident behind the wheel and haven't stopped learning new things. I know that there are many more polished TV presenters than me, and while there's still an element of me turning up each day and thinking I'm going to get found out, I feel more confident in my own skin than I used to. People sometimes ask me if I feel like I've got imposter syndrome. Have I heck! I did have imposter syndrome when I was playing cricket. I'd look around the dressing room, consider the great players who played for England before me and feel like I shouldn't be spoken about in the same breath as them. That's because playing sport is a quantifiable skill. But when it comes to TV, I look around and think, 'Why should I not be doing this?' Not because I'm very good, but simply because if they can do it, why can't I? I'm all over it, don't worry about that.

I'd never really watched anything I'd done, including playing cricket. The thought of sitting there watching myself on TV always just seemed a bit weird. But the kids are now at that age when they want to sit and watch stuff as a family, including anything I'm in, so I don't have much of a choice. Sometimes it's embarrassing because I'll be dressed in drag or performing as a Chippendale on *A League of Their Own*. But mostly when I'm watching *Top Gear*, I cringe and think, 'That's not you, stop presenting!' But I'm a lot more comfortable than I used to be. Viewers seem to like people who throw themselves into things, and that's how I see it, as an opportunity to do stuff that most people would never get the chance to do.

My kids will sometimes say to me, 'Dad, what did you do today?'

'Oh, I just rolled a funeral hearse.'

'Where are you going next week?'

'Nepal.'

I think in some ways they think I'm a bit of an embarrassing dad, and in other ways they enjoy the fact I do a different job to most dads.

CHAPTER TWO

'INFLUENCERS' AND THE INTERNET

I use social media when I have to, mainly when I'm promoting things I've done. I'll think about things I posted in the past and think, 'Why am I doing this for?' I suppose that's the $64,000 question – what is the point of social media?

There was a time, not too long ago, when people didn't feel the need to show or tell anyone anything. Maybe if you'd been on holiday and your mates were round, you'd show them a few photos. But even that was considered a bit naff. And pre-Facebook and Twitter and Instagram and everything else, if people didn't like something they saw on TV or read in a newspaper, they'd maybe have a moan to whoever happened to be sitting next to them. They didn't phone up their mates and shout their opinions down the phone. That would have been seen as weird. But now, people feel the need to share everything about their lives with complete strangers, whether it's their view on the latest news or videos of their cat falling off a tumble dryer. If your cat fell off a tumble dryer pre-social media, you might have told your wife in passing and she might have smiled. Now, it might get thousands of likes from people you don't know and will never meet.

Facebook and Instagram are filtered versions of people's lives. Sometimes literally. People in the social media age want to project a perfect existence. Look at my perfect kids, look at my perfect house, look at my perfect garden, look at my perfect holiday. It's effectively showing off, which used to be frowned upon in society. When I was growing up, parents used to tell their kids off for showing off. Now the parents are showing the kids off on Facebook. All the time. I've even read stories about kids rebelling against their parents because they're being used as tools by so-called internet influencers. What the hell's an influencer? How many followers do you need to be considered an influencer? Is there a guild of influencers? Is there an influencers' union? And why do people take any notice? Whatever the answers, influencers exist, and apparently they're influencing people. It's bonkers.

The madder the online world becomes, and the more people get sucked into its vortex, the more I find myself trying to withdraw from it. I feel like someone on a big ship, jumping overboard before it hits an iceberg. Or someone staggering inside from a snowstorm and locking every door and window. I think lots of people are thinking the same. Don't get me wrong, everywhere I go I see people glued to their phones. Walk around Manchester and you're dodging people all the time, because they've got their heads down and are tapping away as they're strolling. People just cannot bear to be away from their phones for more than a couple of minutes. But I've heard about people giving up their smartphones and going back to one of those old Nokias that can just make calls and send texts. They've got that Snake game, but that's about it.

There have been periods when my alarm would go off in the morning and I'd snooze it and snooze it and snooze it, before thinking, 'Right, that's enough snoozing, time for some social media.' Then I'd roll on my back, press a few buttons on my phone and suddenly I'd be scrolling through Twitter. I'd spend the next half an hour looking at what people I didn't even know were doing or thinking. I'd feel under pressure to follow people I kind of knew, there would be people asking if I'd follow them, and I'd be thinking, 'Well, no. Because I genuinely do not give a shit what you do or think about anything!' Then I'd move onto Rightmove or Auto Trader, to see if any new houses had come on the market or anyone was selling any nice cars. And this would be before I'd even got out of bed. Why? It's not like I needed a new house or a new car or a new anything else, or needed to know what was going on in anyone else's life or what their views were on the Tories or Labour or someone losing weight or putting weight on or saying the wrong thing or saying the right thing in slightly the wrong way. I delete all my social media apps every now and again before getting a new gig and being told to go back on it. I had to go back on Twitter before *Top Gear* started, but I made sure I had to go through all the rigmarole of searching for Twitter on Google and signing in before posting anything.

When you see how much time you spend looking at screens, it's shocking. I see dads sitting in cafes with their kids, staring at their phone, probably scrolling through Facebook, and not talking – I've done it. And I dread to think how some kids are going to turn out, because while I can remember a time when the internet didn't exist – and know it was perfectly fine – they don't know any different. I went to a wedding recently and these kids on another table sat watching their iPads all the way through. It might have been all right if they'd all been watching the same thing on the same iPad, but they weren't. I understand that parents need to have distraction tactics up their sleeves, but part of growing up should be learning to interact with people you don't know, dealing with boredom or being places you don't really want to be. But now I fear kids are growing up with no social skills and instead are being taught that it's acceptable to zone out and ignore everything that's going on around them. It doesn't take a genius to work out that that's promoting selfish, anti-social behaviour. And it's why kids can't hold a conversation and look you in the eye when they speak to you. Instead of sitting there on their iPads watching *Finding Nemo* again, they should be running around outside with a ball, getting muddy.

Mind you, I've not got much tolerance for other people's misbehaving children, so maybe it was best they were watching *Finding Nemo* at the wedding. Luckily, most of the kids who come round my house are good, because if they do stuff I don't like, I won't hesitate to tell them. You have to, don't you? Obviously, there's not a lot you can do about crying babies. It's a nightmare on trains, especially when they're wriggling and kicking and punching things, but you just have to give the parent that little smile and nod that says, 'Don't worry, I understand.' A few years ago, we were coming back from America and my middle lad, who must have been about 18 months at the time, started crying while the plane was getting off the ground. He must have been crying for ten minutes, tops, but the bloke behind us started getting all uppity and whinging to the steward. So I said to her, 'If he carries on complaining, I'm going to say something to him.' She pleaded with me not to and explained that she'd seen it before, that the bloke was planning to use my crying baby to get his money back for his business-class ticket. I felt like saying to him, 'If you don't want to pay for a business-class seat, go and sit in the back!'

Has social media made people angrier or does it just mean there are more platforms for the angry people who already existed to vent? I think social media has made it more acceptable to be angry, so that you're almost seen as odd if you're not. The attitude used to be, 'Oh, no point getting het up. What good will it do?' So you'd just keep it to yourself. But now people feel entitled to whinge and moan and bitch about everything. It's almost become compulsory for people to vent. I don't get it. If you don't like someone or something on TV, don't watch it. Just turn the channel over. If a company has provided you with poor service, get in touch with them privately and tell them how annoyed you are, don't tell everyone else about it. Why do they want to know that the food on your flight from Manchester to Malaga was appalling or your internet has been running a bit slow? Recently, I came close to doing exactly that. I ordered some food from a local Japanese restaurant and only one katsu curry turned up instead of two. I was fuming, like you would not believe. So I phoned the restaurant up and said, 'Look, bit of an issue, one of our katsu curries hasn't turned up.'

'Sorry, sir, we'll refund you.'

'No. I don't want the nine quid back. One of my kids hasn't got any dinner. I just want another katsu curry. Can you please just send it?'

'Oh, we can't do that. They're not our drivers, they're Deliveroo's. You'll have to phone them up.'

'I'm going to stop you right there. Do you think that's right? I'm here trying to eat my food before it gets cold and you're telling me I've also got to chase Deliveroo because the food I ordered from you hasn't turned up.'

'We've had problems like this before, Deliveroo drivers eating the food ...'

'Oh, come on!'

These people have the amazing ability to turn you into a sitcom character, like Basil Fawlty or Alan Partridge, getting incredibly angry about the most trivial of things. So I got straight on the phone to Deliveroo and tried not to rant at some poor bastard at the other end who had nothing to do with anything: 'Have a word with Miso Tasty, they're saying your driver has eaten our food. Send me my katsu curry!' They agreed to send me another one, but I kept getting these messages every half an hour: 'Your food will be with you at 8.30 ... your food will be with you at 9.00 ... your food will be with you at 9.30 ...' By midnight, the katsu curry still hadn't turned up. I was so livid, I very nearly took to social media to tell the world about my katsu curry disaster, before getting a grip and telling myself that there are wars going on in the world, famines, people dying of cancer and animals going extinct. And that's the really sad part about social media: someone famous can post about their katsu curry not turning up and it will start trending in Wales, but when you're trying to raise awareness about an important issue hardly anyone is interested. What does that say about society? It doesn't say anything good, and I have done this in the past too.

I find the competitive element of social media – the ravenous desire for likes and retweets and thumbs up and smiley faces and emojis blowing kisses – just weird and incredibly needy. And why do people equate having lots of followers with being a good person or being successful? That's a terrible message for kids to be absorbing, this idea that goodness or success is all to do with how many likes your posts get. I mean, Hitler had a lot of followers back in the day, but I don't think anyone would argue that made him a good lad. And while he was successful in his own way for a while, things didn't turn out great for him.

A lot of it is to do with entitlement. I see it all the time where I live. It's about wanting to be rewarded for not really doing anything. If people can get followers and likes and attention and make money out of posing in a bikini or drinking a protein shake or a cocktail in some bar on Instagram, then they'll do it. Why would they want to graft when they can ponce around all day doing nothing? That's why it's so irritating when you hear the government calling midwives, nurses and other NHS staff 'low-skilled' workers. Low-skilled? These are some of the most skilled people I've ever met, both technically and emotionally. When Rachael had our fourth child, the baby spent a couple of nights in the intensive care unit and I was in awe of these people. And I can only hope that they get so much satisfaction from doing their jobs, and are rewarded in ways most people can't understand, that it trumps the money they're paid. Because if they're meant to be low-skilled, God knows what that makes the cast of *Made in Chelsea*, and they're all loaded.

It makes no sense. Then again, and it would be remiss of me not to mention it, I am 42.

Why do people feel the need to be bothered about stuff? Something will happen on the other side of the world and everyone will be straight on social media, imploring everyone else to 'pray for this' and 'pray for that'. If they want to say a prayer, why don't they just say one in their bedroom? Or someone famous will die and people will be all over Twitter, telling him or her to rest in peace (why 'rest in peace'? Why not 'rest lively' or 'rest with a bit of vigour'?) or they'll write very long tributes on Instagram, despite never having known them. Everyone feels the need to make themselves so busy nowadays. And then I'll stumble onto Twitter, completely unaware of what's gone on or who's died, write something about *Top Gear* being on this Saturday, and people will start having a go at me for my lack of sensitivity: 'How dare you talk about *Top Gear* at this time?' Hang on a minute, I've never heard of this person who's died. If social media is still around when I die, don't bother paying any tributes. I'm not interested and you probably didn't know me, so talk about something else.

People I actually knew have died and I've thought, 'I should probably say something, shouldn't I? Shall I put an #RIP on Twitter?' Of course, the right thing to do is call the person's loved ones or send them a letter or an email. But if I don't acknowledge their death on social media, I'll get chastised for it. My grandpa was 92 during the coronavirus lockdown, so I was going to put a message on Instagram, wishing him a happy birthday and also saying, 'If anyone knows him, do us a favour and give him a ring.' But then I thought, 'Why does anyone else need to see me wishing my grandpa happy birthday? And he's 92, he'll get pissed off with everyone phoning him all day.' So I just phoned him up instead.

When Alastair Cook retired, the Professional Cricketers' Association put a video together of players congratulating Alastair on a great career, and asked me to appear in it.

I said to them, 'I've already sent him a video message.'

'But what about appearing in our video as well?'

'But I've already congratulated him, personally.'

'Can we post your video message?'

'No! I sent the message to him. Why do I need anyone else to see it?'

As far as I was concerned, I'd done what I needed to do. Why was it important for anyone else to know that I'd congratulated Alastair Cook? But I started questioning myself. Maybe it was important for other people to know that I'd congratulated Alastair Cook. Maybe, according to the modern rules, it made me a bad person that I didn't want other people to see me congratulating Alastair Cook. And then Rob Key texted saying, 'It's only you and Kevin Pietersen who haven't done it.' I replied, 'But I've sent him a message!' Who was this message supposed to be for anyway? Me or Alastair? I was so confused. Kev probably did the same.

People sometimes say to me, 'Why are you not on social media much?' People think it's weird that I don't post every cough and spit of my life. But it's not compulsory, you don't have to do it. And I've done something like 12,000 tweets in the last 12 years – is that not enough? I've got mental health issues but compared to some of the people I see posting on Twitter who don't seem to think there's anything wrong with them, I'm right as rain. Social media highlights people's need to be liked or noticed or, if they're celebrities, stay relevant. I think for some people it's a form of therapy, whether consciously or not. I don't need or even want people to know what I think or what I'm doing.

When my fourth child was born, I didn't tell anyone about it apart from family. I did an interview in Australia for *Ninja Warrior* and the bloke said, 'I understand your wife is expecting your fourth child', and I replied, 'Yeah, it'll be brilliant when it happens.' The fact was, he was already about three months old. I just didn't think that anyone apart from family needed to know about it.

The really strange thing about social media is that celebrities fought for privacy for years, and now they're choosing to just give everything away. And when they post something on social media that gets them into trouble, they're surprised. They don't seem to understand that that was part of the reason why celebrities fought for privacy in the first place. People will hammer you if you say something you're not 'supposed' to, do something you're not 'supposed' to or look how you're not 'supposed' to while out walking the dog. When it comes to social media, famous people can control the message to a certain extent but many of them have learned that they can't have their cake and eat it.

The internet can be a nightmare for people with addictions, whether you're addicted to gambling, sex or Nike Air Jordans. I recently did a documentary for the BBC about eating disorders in men, because I've had one since I can't even remember. I interviewed this lad called Daniel and he told me about the evils of target marketing. Every time you go on the internet and log onto a new site, a banner will pop up and ask if you want to 'accept cookies'. Most people just say yes, without even knowing what cookies are. What they should know is that these cookies store user data and behaviour information, which allows companies to target certain people with advertising. So when Daniel had bulimia, he'd get bombarded with adverts for diets and gyms, which for some people with eating disorders is a dangerous trigger. I think that's the biggest issue with the internet, how it steals people's privacy. People aren't allowed to slip into your house uninvited and rifle through your letters and books while making notes of your interests.

On top of all that, what are all these radio waves doing to us? I know the links between 5G and radiation have been debunked, despite what Eamonn Holmes and David Icke said about it spreading coronavirus, but we don't really know about the long-term damage that all these waves are doing to us. Everywhere you go now, you're surrounded by electrical devices that must be giving things off. You sleep next to your phone, you sit in an office all day surrounded by computers or sit at home tapping away at a laptop. And where are those things that these devices are giving off going? They must be going through people. I reckon we're a massive experiment, like frogs in boiling water, and that we won't really know what all this invisible technology is doing to us until it's too late. In 20 or 30 years, we'll all be running around shouting, 'Hellfire! Everyone's dying of Wi-Fi!' If not that, then it will be something else.

Has the internet improved my life? I'm sure it has in some ways, although I'm struggling to think of any. It basically makes it easier to do things that weren't that difficult to do in the first place. Like walking to the shops or getting a map out of the glovebox. In fact, let's not beat around the bush, the internet has been a bit of a nightmare for society. When it first came along, everyone was blown away by the fact that suddenly all this information was at your fingertips. But it's gone too far the other way. I've realised that mankind's thirst for information means that people feel the need to be connected to the internet for hours at a time. I'll be on Instagram or Facebook and think to myself, 'What am I doing? Why am I bothered that someone I don't really know is having a barbecue?' I'm genuinely not bothered, which is the really strange part about it. Sometimes before I go to bed, I check how much time I've spent looking at my screen and it's horrifying. Some days, I'll have spent four or five hours looking at my screen, and my life won't be any better for it. I'll even make excuses for my behaviour, like the fact I also use my phone as a remote control, but I'm just kidding myself. And if the internet is bad for adults, it's far worse for kids. There's so much on there that they really shouldn't be seeing and you can't get them off it. And it creates so much stress, because they're constantly wanting to know if something they've posted on Instagram or Snapchat has been liked or commented on.

One thing the internet has done lately is give me a trainer addiction, to add to the Nutella addiction I've been unable to shake. I don't know where it came from, but I suddenly found myself buying a pair of Nike Air Jordans. Then I bought another pair. And another. Now I can't help myself. I must have bought 30 pairs of trainers in the first few months of 2020. I'm on loads of different websites, all of which send me alerts when a new pair drops. If you're on the ball when there's a drop, you might pay £150 for a pair. But because they might only be dropping a limited amount of that model, the following day sites will be selling them for four or five hundred quid. I've got a trainer mate called Howard, who cuts my hair. Whenever there's a drop, we'll text each other, because it's likely that both of us didn't manage to get a pair. Unfortunately, he's only a size eight. Some of these trainers can go for thousands of pounds. And they're not made of gold or anything, just leather and plastic. I'm telling you, these Nike and Adidas trainers are like the new modern art or fine wine.

Last year, I was filming *A League of Their Own* and Jamie Redknapp got this lad to come in and sell some trainers. I picked out a few pairs for me and my kids, thinking that they were maybe a hundred quid max. But when I got the bill through, they were a few hundred quid each, because apparently they were designed by Kanye West. I've never worn mine. I want to wear them, but I like them too much. They're still in boxes in my wardrobe, with the paper wrapping. Every now and again, I'll take a pair out. I forget what I've got, so I'll be holding them up to the light, turning them around as if they're ancient relics and saying, 'Oh, I forgot I had these ones. What a pair of beauties.' And while I'm looking at them, I'll be wearing a pair of shit trainers that I've had for years.

I did wear a pair of them once, when I was filming *Ninja Warrior* in Australia. What a mistake that was. I was standing on the sidelines, minding my own business, when one of the production executives stood on my pure white trainers and said, 'Good luck.'

It reminds me of when my grandparents used to put plastic covers on their couches. I'd think, 'Why would you keep the seats nice for the next person? Why don't you just enjoy them yourselves?' When I'm 70, either I'll have a massive collection of valuable antique trainers to flog or I'll be rocking about in these retro trainers, the coolest pensioner in England. That's if my lads don't go rogue and nick them in the meantime. One of them is nearly my size already and he's only 14. I might have to get a padlock for my wardrobe.

CHAPTER THREE

THE PRESTON PATRIOT

I went to a couple of St George's Day celebrations years ago and they made me wince, because they were bordering on xenophobic. They'd bring these big roasts out, salute them and saw them up, before getting people up to rant and rave about what England meant to them. That's all fine in theory, but what they thought England should be was like a vision from the 1960s. England has moved on, it's a multicultural country now, just like almost every country in western Europe and the developed world. When it comes to most things, I'd argue that personal opinions can't be wrong, because they're personal opinions. But racism and xenophobia are just wrong, end of story.

England shouldn't still be defined by a couple of wars we won in the early twentieth century or by whiteness, we should recognise that people from all over the world enhance the country. Nothing is going to change, the world is a global village, and has been for decades. I liked the fact that when I was growing up, my dad had mates from India, Pakistan and the Caribbean. I'm lucky in that from an early age, I never saw colour in the same way a lot of people my age did and I thought a multicultural society is what England should be. I've never been able to get my head around how anyone could automatically regard someone of a different colour or nationality or religion as problematic. The nice thing about kids is they don't even see any differences.

I think it's a shame that people aren't proud of being English. I think you can reject all that jingoism and suspicion of foreigners and still be a 'good' patriot. I've never really considered myself to be European, which is what a lot of people started saying they were after Brexit kicked off, and I see myself as English rather than British. That's not because I don't like Europe or the other countries that make up Britain – and I wanted to remain in Europe – it's just because I'm proud to be English, which is probably connected to the fact I represented England at cricket. It makes me sad that our manufacturing has collapsed and you can't buy much that was made in England any more. I'd like to be able to buy things from England. I don't think that's narrow-minded or bigoted, that's just natural, because it's good for all English people. Even having to make excuses for being proud of being English now. That's how it is, and it's ridiculous.

I don't like it when people knock England, just as I don't like it when people knock Lancashire or Preston, because it's where I'm from. When I go back to Preston now, I feel a real sense of belonging. Recently, I was doing some filming on my old estate and I felt right at home. I got chatting to these kids who were pulling wheelies on their bikes, the sort of kids a lot of people would avoid, just because of the way they look. They were great, nothing like the way they're stereotyped, and talking to them made me quite nostalgic.

I think it might be slightly different if you're from a northern town, because different towns and regions down south don't tend to have their own accents, they've all merged into one. I don't think I've got much of a Preston accent any more. I noticed that when I was chatting to those kids on the estate and Natalie in the chippy, I didn't sound like them at first. But I soon slipped back into it, so much so that it became a bit of a struggle for the southern film crew, that was for sure. However, you can travel 20 minutes down the road, to Bolton or Wigan or St Helens, and the accent will change completely. That gives you a real sense that you're part of a community with its own identity, shared past and traditions, separate from anywhere else.

Parts of Preston might not look that promising, with each estate looking like the next, and I know some pretty dodgy stuff goes on there. But at least everyone knows and looks out for each other. I've met my next-door neighbours in Cheshire, but I don't know anyone else on my road. And people don't really look out for each other in Cheshire, they mainly want to tell me how fast their car goes or where they're going on their holidays. In Preston, you can have normal conversations with people. It's not superficial, people ask you how you are and what you've been up to and you can tell there's a genuine interest. When I was still drinking, I'd pop into a fancy bar and get looked after really well, but only because they thought it was nice to have someone vaguely famous in the place.

I don't speak French or Italian, so I don't know if French people or Italians spend all day on social media slagging off their own countries. But they can't be as bad as English people. Americans love being Americans, Aussies love being Aussies, Kiwis love being Kiwis. And I guarantee that you will never meet a Scottish or Welsh person who feels uncomfortable about being proud of their country. They celebrate being from where they are. But if you read some of these comments on social media, you'd think England was the worst country in the world.

A lot of it stems from guilt. We spent a few hundred years conquering other countries and building this massive empire and, unsurprisingly, it didn't go down too well with many of the locals. And now that's come home to roost. We caused so much chaos and suffering that it's now seen as problematic to celebrate Englishness. I can totally understand that, because I read about some of the things the English did and think, 'Jesus, what the hell were they thinking? How could they be so horrible? Who thought it was a good idea to rock up to Africa and make people slaves?' But it wasn't me. I had nothing to do with the subjugation of India or the Opium Wars with China. And it wasn't just the English, it was French, the Spanish, the Italians, the Germans, the Belgians and just about every other country in western Europe. That's what European countries did back then, went around nicking other people's lands.

When someone asks me what it means to be English, I find it difficult to answer. English culture is a slippery thing because we're so diverse now. But I think it's a good thing that English culture is difficult to describe, because that suggests it's dynamic and always changing. And if I had to say what the best thing about England and Britain was, it would be its inclusivity. I've been to a lot of places that cling onto their culture and national identity, to the exclusion of newcomers. I wouldn't want to live in a country like that. I went to Oktoberfest in Munich and couldn't believe how white it was. It made me feel uncomfortable. We had an Asian lad as part of the production team and people were staring at him. Then they'd look at me as if to say, 'You're one of us', and I'd be thinking, 'No, I'm not!' That's the thing about Germany, they're a very proud country and retain a lot of their old traditions, despite the part they played in the Second World War. They don't seem to be embarrassed, and that was less than 100 years ago. Maybe that's because they lost? Maybe the fact we won is a problem, because it means people keep going on about it and wanting to define us by how we were in the 1940s, and other people are turned off by that.

I suppose it's about finding a balance: retaining old traditions while managing to incorporate the traditions of immigrants. Food is a great example. For years, England and Britain were famous for having bad food. Even in the 1990s, French president Jacques Chirac was making jokes about British food being the worst in the world – apart from Finnish. But London is now one of the world's gastronomical hotspots. That's because we started with a blank slate. Now, we've got the lot: traditional British food that has been made sophisticated, and food from just about every country in the world. In Spanish cities, for example, it's mainly Spanish food. That's great if you want to eat Spanish food all the time, but it's not so great if you don't.

Sometimes, it's difficult to know whether you're allowed to like certain historical English figures or not. Every country has historical figures that are problematic by modern standards.

I've been to Buckingham Palace and met the Queen, and while I wouldn't say I was overwhelmed, it did make me feel special in some way. I suppose that feeling was pride. But was it pride at my personal achievement or pride at doing what I did for my country? It's difficult to say. But that was the Queen, who is an amazing woman. She's tiny but has an aura like no one else I've met.

I can understand why a lot of people think the royal family are a waste of money. Let's face it, they haven't exactly been covering themselves in glory these past few decades, and now we've got Prince Harry resigning and Prince Andrew being accused of all sorts and claiming it can't have been him because he doesn't sweat and was having dinner in Pizza Express in Woking. They're in a bit of a pickle, no doubt about that, but I don't agree with getting rid of them. They bring so much money into the country, in terms of trade and tourism, that we should keep them for financial reasons, if no other. People say we could get rid of the royal family while keeping the palaces and parks and what not, but how would that work? What about all the money that gets made when one of them gets married or has a kid? And what would be the point of Buckingham Palace if the Queen didn't live there? It wouldn't make sense. Then again, when the Queen goes, that will be the turning point for a lot of people. Say what you like about the Queen, she's kind of impossible to hate. But Charles comes with a lot of baggage and is not everyone's cup of tea.

Funnily enough, I met Meghan a few years ago. I'd had a massive night out and was sleeping off my hangover on the sofa in my agent's office. He came in and said, 'Right, you have to get out now, I've got a meeting with this girl off *Suits*.' I found a sofa in another office and saw her walk in with a press pack and some books. Apparently, Richard had to say to her, 'I don't know what I can do for you.' But it turned out she had bigger fish to fry.

I even felt awkward singing 'God Save the Queen' before matches, although that was mainly because we'd have to do it at 10.30 in the morning when there were only about 50 people in the stands and everyone could hear me. It's not as if I didn't like the anthem, I just thought it was unnecessary for a cricket match. In America, they sing it before everything, and if anyone doesn't stand up or put their hand on their heart, people think they're wrong 'uns. And I've seen plenty of people start crying when they've won a gold medal at the Olympics and their country's flag is being hauled up the pole. But that was never going to be me. I'm patriotic and could get a bit emotional, but I was never a blubberer. That was fine with me, because some of the people who did put their hand on their heart and get a bit teary weren't patriotic, they just looked it. When I started playing for England, we were rubbish. We shouldn't have been, because we had some good players. But a more selfish group of players the world has never seen. They weren't patriots, they were narcissists. Patriotism is about playing well, so that the England team win.

CHAPTER FOUR

THE STATE OF CRICKET

Imagine if cricket didn't already exist and someone came along and tried to invent it. Imagine the conversations with broadcasters and members of the public: 'So, there are two teams of 11 players and they both take it in turns to bat and bowl. There are two players batting at the same time, and their main aim is to stop the ball hitting three pieces of wood sticking out of the ground. In one-day cricket, they bat and bowl once. And a one-day game can go on for 20 overs, 40 overs or 50 overs. I'll explain what an over is in a minute. But in first-class cricket, they have to bat and bowl twice. But the only people who'll be able to watch that are pensioners, the unemployed or the unemployable, because it's played during the week, when most people are at work. If it's a first-class match between two countries, the game can go on for five days. That's called a Test.

If it does last the full five days, it's a draw. But it might not last five days, it might last only three or four. Sometimes less. And because people don't really expect a game to last four or five days, the ground will often be full for the first three days. Bit weird, I know, but that's just the way we've designed it, so that people flock to watch the result being set up but hardly anyone watches the game being won. And when the winning team are celebrating, the cheers are literally echoing around the ground. If they're celebrating winning a series – I'll come back to that – they'll be spraying champagne at each other and feeling a bit stupid, because it doesn't feel like anyone else is particularly interested. And if it rains you can't play. Instead, the players sit in a pavilion getting bored and the fans huddle under stair-cases drinking very expensive beer and burgers. But you don't rearrange the game for another time, you pretend like it never happened. Did I mention that a Test series might consist of five games and last for months? No? I'm not quite finished yet. Not interested? Oh, fair enough, I'll try someone else ...'

What kind of state is cricket in? It depends on what you're comparing it to. If you're comparing it to shove ha'penny, then it's flying. If you're comparing it to football, then it's in a terrible state. But most sports all over the world are in a terrible state compared to football. Football is the benchmark in terms of playing numbers, attendances, fandom, money and media attention, and every other sport is fighting for little scraps. There was a time, not so long ago, when that wasn't the case. Back in the 1980s, you'd even get snooker on the back pages of the tabloids instead of football. But now, probably the only sport that can shift football is boxing (and only if Anthony Joshua or Tyson Fury are fighting) or rugby union (and only if England are doing well in a World Cup). Obviously, English cricket has had its moment in the sun since, for example the 2005 Ashes and when the national team won the World Cup in such dramatic fashion in 2019, but I suspect they were blips rather than part of a trend. As things stand, English cricket is where it has been for many years, a second- or possibly third-tier sport.

When kids reach 14 or 15, and realise that they don't want to spend all week working hard at school only to spend all weekend playing cricket because they've got mates to mess around with and girls to chase and any number of other things to do, they start drifting off. Cricket is also an expensive game. Modern bats cost a few hundred quid (and break far more easily than old ones, despite not being guaranteed) and there's also the gloves and pads and other protective equipment to consider. And a lot of state schools don't play it because they don't have access to equipment or pitches or nets or groundsmen, which is why there are fewer working-class players in county cricket than there were 100 years ago. Gone are the days when, as the old saying goes, the committees of some counties only had to whistle down the pit shaft to summon a handful of fast bowlers. If the England team has a bad few years when they're getting thumped by the Aussies and not winning trophies, cricket's relevance could slide even further.

Whether you think cricket is healthy or not also depends on what you want it to look like. I want Test cricket to be strong, I want England to be good at it and I want the Ashes to be massive. That's because I think Test cricket is and always should be the pinnacle. But even I realise that that's an outdated way of looking at the situation. In England, we still get big crowds for Test cricket, but that isn't the case in other parts of the world. In some countries, Test cricket seems to be hanging on for dear life. I watch Test matches in the West Indies or Sri Lanka and there's hardly anyone there, even on day one. Then again, people were going on about Test cricket hanging on for dear life when I started playing. Even 20 years ago, the bulk of the crowd for Tests would be English, apart from in Australia, where Test cricket still has huge cultural significance.

One of English cricket's biggest problems is its lack of visibility, in that it's no longer shown live on terrestrial TV. If huge swathes of the population without satellite subscriptions can't watch it, they're not going to be into it. The 2005 Ashes series, which was broadcast by Channel 4, was watched by millions and made players household names. But it wasn't sustainable, for Channel 4 or English cricket. Since taking over, Sky has invested hundreds of millions of pounds into English cricket. Without that money, I'm not sure English cricket would be as healthy as it is today. So how can people say Sky have been bad for cricket? It doesn't really make sense. Who would be showing cricket if Sky weren't? Do people really think that BBC2 would clear eight hours a day for five days for a Test match between

England and Bangladesh? And do they really think that the money the BBC would pay would prop up English cricket? Pay TV has been necessary to keep the game afloat. And Sky's coverage is brilliant, they've brought it such a long way in the last 20 years.

Cricket has been transitioning for quite a while now, basically since the introduction of Twenty20 at the start of the century. Twenty20 has changed the game in many ways, from the way it's played to the priorities of players, fans and broadcasters. If you're a kid now, you don't want to watch a batsman score a careful 50 from 150 balls, even if it's for the good of the team. Kids don't watch that and think, 'Wow, what a craftsman, what technique, what patience and concentration', they just think it's boring. Instead, they want to see someone come out and smash 50 from 15 balls. And a lot of today's players are the same. I'll hear them waxing lyrical about the Big Bash in Australia or the Indian Premier League (IPL) or the Bangladesh Premier League or read their social-media posts about how far they or someone else belted a ball, and not be able to get my head around it. Some of these lads will be good players making a decent living, which I can't blame them for. But we now have the situation where players who work hard to be what used to be called 'proper' batsmen – players like Kent and England's Zak Crawley, who can get his head down and grind out innings against good fast bowling – are earning far less money than Twenty20 specialists who travel the world trying to belt every ball as far as they can, which is dangerous for the longer forms of the game.

As soon as the authorities, broadcasters, sponsors and rich businessmen realised that young people prefer to watch bowlers being smashed all over the park for a few hours than a life and death struggle between bat and ball, that spelled trouble for longer forms of the game. The Indian Premier League turned everything on its head because of the amount of money involved and the glamour associated with it. Suddenly, there were billionaires and movie stars involved in cricket, the sport seemed sexier, the fans lapped up the razzmatazz and players became rich beyond their wildest dreams.

When I started playing cricket, hardly any cricketers were rich. I certainly didn't expect to make my fortune playing cricket. My biggest ambition was to play Test cricket for England, and the old-fashioned way was to graft in domestic cricket, score lots of runs, get picked by your country, make a name for yourself on the international stage and then earn a load of cash playing Twenty20 for a few years at the end, almost as a bonus. But I suspect we'll start seeing younger players taking a different route: playing loads of Twenty20, lapping up the glitz and glamour, making a load of cash and hoping that that will be a route into the England set-up. And if it isn't a route into the England set-up, at least they might be financially secure.

The IPL and Twenty20 in general reflect modern society. I look at Twenty20 like *Love Island*. To get invited onto *Love Island*, people don't have to do anything other than look good. And once they're on it, they don't have to do anything other than look good and be slightly amusing for a few weeks. Twenty20 cricket is similar. Players who aren't even that good can get picked up by an IPL team and earn a lot of money for playing one or two decent innings. They might be the next big thing for five minutes, but at the end of their career hardly anyone will remember them. They'll just be one of hundreds of IPL players who smashed a few sixes one night in Mumbai or Chennai or Jaipur for some team or other that they didn't even have any connection to, other than the fact their owner decided to buy them at an auction, usually because some other rich person had bought a player they wanted. There are cricketers who are brilliant in all forms of the game, but they won't be remembered for what they did for the Rajasthan Royals or Sunrisers Hyderabad, they'll be remembered for the great things they did for their countries in Test matches or World Cups, whether it's Ben Stokes for England, Steve Smith for Australia or even India's own Virat Kohli.

But even I realise that saying that Tests are the ultimate form for cricket comes with a bit of snobbery. West Indies cricket was in a terrible place for years and years. They went from being the most powerful Test team in the world in the early 1990s to also-rans in the space of less than a decade. Kids fell out of love with it and they stopped producing world-class players, I suspect because people who might have been batsmen concentrated on football instead and people who might have been fast bowlers concentrated on basketball. But the fact there has been a bit of a resurgence in West Indies cricket is down to Twenty20. Players like Chris Gayle, who was probably the most famous Twenty20 player in the world for a few years, made cricket attractive again, the West Indies won a couple of World Cups and you could argue that without Twenty20, cricket would be on life support in the Caribbean. I'm not sure if the West Indies will ever be a force in Test cricket again, but if you're winning Twenty20 World Cups, does it really matter? Then when you go to India, cricket there is like football is here, except maybe bigger. And Indian cricketers who make a name for themselves in the IPL earn more than Premier League footballers. Once they retire from cricket, they never have to work again. People argue that Twenty20 has ruined the delicate balance between bat and ball, but I wouldn't worry about that. There are lots of problems with cricket, but I've never been one to complain about wickets being too flat and bowlers not having enough assistance. There were periods in history when bowlers had the edge, and now batsmen have got the upper hand. Fans have always liked to see runs, so we should give them what they want. The challenge for bowlers is to learn new things and be more skilful.

Far more of a worry than international cricket is first-class domestic cricket. The County Championship actually costs the counties money to play it, because hardly anyone watches it. How long can that carry on? It makes no sense. If hardly anyone watches something, year after year, the only rational thing to do is to stop doing it. Surely at some point in the not-too-distant future, someone will take over the domestic game – some innovative thinker, who's maybe only a young kid now – and think, 'Hang on a minute, I'm all for tradition, but if the County Championship is being played to empty grounds, what's the point of it? Who's it aimed at? Why are we spending money to keep this afloat when we could be playing Twenty20 cricket – which people watch and makes money – all the time instead? And players now get selected for England on T20 form.' That's when massive changes will take place, not just in England but all over the world. The purists will dig in and fight, but the changes might just save the game and assure its future.

No other branch of the entertainment industry would continue doing the same thing if hardly anyone was interested and it was losing money. If hardly anyone was watching *Top Gear*, they'd pull the plug mid-series. If a musical in the West End was only 10 per cent full every night, it wouldn't last a month. If your band went on tour and was playing to a handful of people in arenas, the tour would be cut short and you'd probably break the band up. If the County Championship does ever come to an end, it will be like when old high-street chains like Woolworths go under. Everyone will be running around clutching their heads and crying and shouting about how much they loved it, and when you'll ask them, 'When was the last time you watched a County Championship game?' they'll reply, 'Oh, not since I was a kid', just like people hadn't been to Woolworths for decades. How does it make sense to be upset about losing something you weren't interested in in the first place? I'm interested in county cricket and I like it, but does it make sense?

The County Championship is the worst business proposition imaginable, an almost impossible sell. If you went on *Dragon's*

Den with that idea – 'Right, it's a game that hardly anyone will want to watch in person, which will lose loads of money and will be propped up by TV money, although hardly anyone will want to watch it on TV either, because they're all watching sports that make sense like football instead' – they'd not take you up on the offer. When I played the game, I wanted to win the County Championship so badly. The fact that I didn't still irritates me today.

People sometimes ask me, 'How can we make first-class cricket cooler or sexier?' I'm sorry, but sitting there in the cold at eleven o'clock in the morning watching Derbyshire versus Leicestershire will never be cool or sexy to a lot of people. You can chuck millions of pounds of marketing at it – 'Forget about *Love Island*, get yourselves down to the County Ground in Derby and you might get to see some cricket between the rain!' – but people aren't stupid. Watching Derbyshire versus Leicestershire wasn't even cool or sexy 100 years ago. The difference is, things didn't have to be cool or sexy in days gone by, they could be interesting and complicated and eccentric and that was fine. Now, unless something is marketed as cool or sexy, people think it's a waste of time. Perhaps those people in authority who keep pushing the shorter forms of the game are the wise people and people like me and other ex-players and journalists who think the longer forms of the game are king are delusional.

At least you used to be able to say that the County Championship was a breeding ground for Test cricketers, but even that's not the case any more. Nowadays, someone will score a few runs in Twenty20 cricket, play a few funky shots and hit a few sixes, and everyone will be talking about them playing Test cricket for England. Or a player will be rested for England games and end up playing in the IPL instead, for a lot more money. If someone wants to prioritise playing Twenty20 cricket for franchises all over the world, good luck to them. But if you want to play Test cricket for England, you've got to earn your spot by churning out runs week in, week out in the County Championship and be available when picked. Otherwise, it makes first-class cricket irrelevant.

I'm not sure the cricket authorities really know what they want cricket to be. We've got Twenty20 cricket, 40-over cricket,

50-over cricket, three-day cricket, five-day cricket – which some people think should become four-day cricket. They seem to be chucking as much as they can at a wall and hoping something sticks, and now they've come up with a new tournament called The Hundred. The Hundred has had a lot of criticism from traditionalists, not least because it's set to be played by city-based franchises rather than the traditional counties. But I get what they're trying to do – put on a competition in the summer holidays, when the weather is at its best and families are looking for things to do, broadcast it on the BBC, which has to be a good thing, and build everything else around it. I hope it's a success and I'll do my best to make it one.

Being a cricket presenter isn't necessarily what I want to be, but I felt like I had some sort of responsibility to get involved with The Hundred. There's been unprecedented amounts of money spent on it (although probably not enough to get the Indian lads interested) and if it doesn't work, the repercussions for the game could be terrible. So I think we've all got to try and make it work, even if we might have some misgivings about the tweaks they've made, like introducing city franchises and 10-ball overs. Did I think we needed another format? Probably not. But when all things are said and done, and whatever you want to call it, it's just another game of cricket. It's people bowling and people trying to hit fours and sixes and generally entertain.

I remember when the ECB signed a deal with Ian Stanford for a $20 million Twenty20 match between England and a West Indies XI in 2008 and everyone going on about how it might be the end of cricket as we know it. But as soon as they realised they stood to earn a few quid from it, loads of those ex-players suddenly wanted in on it. Ian Botham came out and said he loved the idea, said Stanford could be great for the game. And then when it all went tits up, he said that the ECB should never have gone along with it. It's funny what money does to people, and we're seeing it with The Hundred. I've had conversations with people who have said how rubbish and pointless it's going to be, and the next week I've found out that they're going to be working on it. Then they're all over the media, telling everyone how it could be the saviour of English cricket. As for the players involved, of course they'll be happy with it, because it means they'll get to bag a few more quid and show off their talents on terrestrial TV.

But something has got to give. It won't be 50-over cricket, because that allows for so much advertising, which funds the game, especially in India. And it won't be Twenty20 cricket, because it's still popular. So I suspect it will be the first-class game. I've always been an advocate for fewer teams playing fewer first-class games of a better standard. That might mean creating regional teams, like the state competition in Australia. Their competition isn't that strong, but if more care was taken over an English regional competition, the standards were high and games were marketed as events, I think it could be a success. Just as important, it would be a far better breeding ground for Test cricketers. But that's not going to happen any time soon, because the people in charge of the counties are incredibly proud to be part of the County Championship and too steeped in tradition to support anything that threatens their existence.

Ultimately, the public decides how successful or out of time something is, and they've been deciding with their feet and remote controls for a long time now. Cricket's fundamental problem is that times have changed. Nothing can survive on tradition and nostalgia alone and almost everything eventually goes out of fashion. Look at snooker: in the 1980s, it was all the rage. Even before he became world champion, Dennis Taylor was a household name mainly because he wore his glasses upside down and Kirk Stephens was rock and roll because he wore a white waistcoat. Now, almost everyone you meet thinks snooker is dull, even though the standard is miles better than it was back then. I'd also argue that the standard of cricket is higher than it was. There are fewer batsmen who can stay at the crease for hours on end, but they have got more skilful and found lots of different ways of scoring runs. For that reason, I'd also say it's a better product than it was. But just as snooker will always be snooker, cricket will always be cricket. Either you'll be into it or you won't, however much they try to dress it up or make it cooler or sexier.

The one thing that leaves me cold about cricket, as it does with all sports, is the fact it's become so tied to technology. I'm not a technophobe, I just think that there's too much technology about that solves problems that don't exist. That sort of technology leaves me cold, whether it's to do with sport, cars or anything really. When I'm driving a fast car, I actually want to be driving it, not the car driving me. I don't want to be looking at a load of touch screens, I just want a speed dial to tell me how fast I'm going and hear the roaring. Too much reliance on technology makes things sterile. Look at Formula 1, it should be the most exciting sport in the world, but an awful lot of people find it dull. In modern sport, there is so much computer analysis and everything is so professional and planned to within an inch of its life, it's almost as if they're trying to take chance out of it. I've always said that sport is an art, not a science. It should be creative and unpredictable, not nerdy and calculated. That's why people love sportspeople who are unconventional and why Tyson Fury is so popular. He's flawed but he's interesting. In fact, he's interesting because he's flawed. He's a free spirit and you're never quite sure what's going to happen when he speaks into a microphone or enters a ring. When he comes on my TV screen, I can't take my eyes off him.

Ben Stokes is similar. He's a brilliant cricketer, but I wouldn't put my house on him. He might walk out and score the best 100 you've ever seen or he might get caught in the slips third ball, having a right go. I'd rather that than watch someone blunt 100 in a day and a half. Not interested. People don't like perfection, which is why when a sportsperson gets too good, the public turns on them. 'Good' becomes synonymous with 'boring'. We've seen it across all sports, from Steve Davis in snooker to Michael Schumacher in Formula 1 to Floyd Mayweather in boxing. Steve Smith is getting to be that way, unless you're Australian. His Test average is 63, so he's going to get at least that whenever he bats. Well done, Steve. I don't like predictability and probably would have hated Don Bradman. Imagine going to watch a cricket match and knowing that someone was probably going to score a 100?

I think Steve Smith is brilliant, as a player and a bloke, and I won't hear a bad word against him. But as I said when I interviewed him in Australia a few years ago, 'Steve, to me you're like beetroot in a sandwich.' He was a bit perplexed, so I had to explain to him that, like beetroot in a sandwich (which Aussies love), he shouldn't really work but he does. As a player, he annoys me so much. I don't know what I'd do if I had to bowl to Steve Smith. I'd probably abuse the shit out of him. I'd have to. And what makes him more annoying is the fact that he doesn't mean to be annoying. Just the way he leaves the ball would drive me round the bend. I wouldn't be able to stop myself having a go at him. But then I'd feel all conflicted, because he's such a nice lad. It's easier to get stuck into someone when you know they're a prick.

Other than the abuse, I'd bowl to him just like any other batter. I'd bowl my best ball, pitch it on or just outside off-stump. Bowlers create more problems for themselves by changing what they usually do to suit him. Just bowl as you normally would and make him hit your best balls. If he's doing that successfully, just try and hit him on the head. Bowl bouncers and set fields for that. But that's easier said than done, because if he started doing that extravagant leave of his, it would wind me up so much. The last person I saw leave a ball like that was England wicketkeeper Jack Russell, and everyone thought he was daft.

Actually, Jack Russell was daft. When I was 17, I was 12th man for Jack and one of my jobs was making his Weetabix at lunch. He gave me strict instructions to put milk on his Weetabix at 1.04, so that they were ready for him when he came off at 1.15. The first two days were fine, but on the third day I put the milk on a bit late. I gave him his Weetabix, he had a taste and said, 'Did you put the milk on a 1.11?

'No, Jack, 1.04, just like you said.'

'You did, didn't you?'

'Yes, Jack. Sorry, Jack, I forgot ...'

Nowadays, I'm always being asked if Ben Stokes is better than I was. Personally, I think it's a bit unfair on Ben, because he's a left-handed batsman and I got left-handed batsmen out in my sleep. Ask Adam Gilchrist and Brian Lara! I'm only joking. Sort of. Let's just say that I was a better bowler than he is and he's a better left-handed batter than me. Saying that, I'd get Ben out every day of the week ... But seriously, as well as being a fine player, Ben now has something that's impossible to quantify: stature. Ian Botham had the same thing, and I had it a little bit. If you considered Ben's bowling in isolation, you'd think it was just all right. He's a decent bowler, because he's quite quick and swings it. However, because it's Ben Stokes bowling those same deliveries, it's a completely different proposition. Whenever Ben comes on to bowl, it's an event. Everyone is thinking, 'Ben Stokes has got the ball in his hands – and he makes things happen.' Botham was the same in the second part of his career. He'd be sending down deliveries at barely 80 mph and getting wickets based on reputation, because batsmen were playing the man rather than the ball. And when Ben walks out to bat, you can almost see the panic on the faces of opposition players. Bowlers will be thinking about doing things differently, instead of doing what they should do, which is bowl their best deliveries.

It's not just cricketers who use their reputation as a weapon. You get comedians who have been around for years and earned the right for people to laugh at them. Their material might not even be funny any more, but people want to laugh at them regardless. Some young comedian might follow them on the stage, have loads of great jokes and not get anywhere near as many laughs, because no one knows who they are. It's the same with old singers, whose voices have cracked and can't reach the notes like they used to. Taken in isolation, their voices are shot to bits. But people still want to hear them, because of how good their voices were in the past.

So when I say that Ben Stokes' ability is bolstered by his reputation, that's not trying to do him down, that's the ultimate compliment. Not many people in this world have that kind of presence. Even when Ben's standing in the field, he has an aura about him. He lets batsmen know he's there, just by the way he carries himself. That's an incredible weapon for a sportsperson to have in their armoury. He still wouldn't get me out though, and if we're going to make this a Top Trumps contest, I reckon I've got him covered when it comes to fielding. He does a lot of diving in the slips, whereas I just stuck my hands out. When it comes to fielding, sometimes less is more. Ben might be more agile and look quicker than me, but I was a chess player, quick in the mind and a few moves ahead. You don't have to be diving anywhere, just read it! And it didn't matter if you stuck me on the boundary, I didn't drop a catch in the outfield between 1998 at Nottingham and the Big Bash in 2013, when

I shelled a skyer. Fifteen years without dropping a ball, I was absolutely gutted.

I had a pretty weird career, in that I was injured for my first 20-odd Test matches. I couldn't bowl properly because of a knackered back and wasn't a good enough batter to make up for it. I had a few years when I was quite useful, including the 2005 Ashes series, before getting injured again. Then I had a couple of good series towards the end of my career, when my bowling was as fast as it had ever been, my batting was coming together a little bit and I honestly thought I was coming into my own as a cricketer. But then injury forced me to retire at 31. So it looks like I never really fulfilled my talent or promise. But my legacy, as people like to call it, is more complicated, in that some people look at my numbers and conclude that I underachieved, while other people get all romantic and conclude that I was better than I was. I'd like to get rid of those 20-odd Tests at the start of my career, because I was rubbish. After that, I was a decent cricketer who had some good days and was usually more influential against better opposition. But I feel uncomfortable when people suggest that

I was a great cricketer. I wasn't, my numbers and averages tell you that. But that doesn't bother me, because I was never just batting or bowling, I was always battling something else, whether it was injuries, depression, an eating disorder or all sorts of other things. So when I look back on my career, I'm actually really proud of it. I think I did all right.

But joking aside, Ben Stokes is a better cricketer than I was, although he's got plenty of work to do to be considered England's greatest ever cricketer. Jimmy Anderson's taken more wickets than any other fast bowler in Test cricket, and while England has produced plenty of excellent players – people like Ben, Ian Botham, Alastair Cook and Graham Gooch – I'd argue that in the modern era, Jimmy is the only Englishman who is a genuine all-time great of world cricket. For what he's done on wickets all over the world, he's right up there with the likes of Glenn McGrath, Curtly Ambrose and Wasim Akram. And he's from Burnley! Ben might get to that level, but he's got Jacques Kallis to aim for, and he scored over 13,000 runs and took 292 wickets in Tests. When Ben retires, I hope he'll be spoken about in the same breath. But to do that, he has to do more than smash it about and score the odd eye-catching 100. He has to be consistent. That's tough for an all-rounder, because it's hardly ever the case that both parts of your game are where you want them to be. If Ben can find that consistency, who knows.

Ben certainly had a fine 2019, what with that incredible match-winning innings in the World Cup final and an excellent Ashes series. I actually did the opening ceremony for the World Cup, which was an absolute shambles and will probably go down as one of the worst moments in television history. We were meant to be broadcasting during breaks in the ceremony, but no one told us, so there was loads of dead air. Paddy McGuinness was trying to speak but didn't have a cameraman and I ended up trying to interview someone I wasn't meant to interview just to fill time (it was actually Pakistani Nobel Laureate Malala Yousafzai, although I didn't know that at the time). The good part was, they gave me five tickets for the final, which meant I finally got to experience what it was like being a cricket fan. I'd often wondered what it must be like sitting in one of those seats, and it turns out it's a bloody long day. The last two hours were amazing, but I had to watch everything else to get to that point. And I did find myself thinking, 'I'd love to be playing in this game.' It's not like I wished I was Ben Stokes, but I did wish I had the opportunity to influence the game in the way he was influencing it. I don't think that will ever go.

As soon as the England lads had lifted the trophy, I had to jump in the car and drive to Scarborough because my boys were playing there for Lancashire. But it was amazing to see England win it in person, because part of me thought it wouldn't happen. I backed them to win it before the tournament, because I'm patriotic and thought they were the best team. But we almost always mess up on the biggest occasions, that's just the English way. So when we got to the final, I thought we were going to get turned over. And I still thought we were going to get turned over until about the last 20 minutes. After that, everything went in our favour. First, Trent Boult caught Ben Stokes but stepped on the rope, and then Ben was awarded another six after a throw ricocheted off his bat and over the boundary. How we won that game I don't know, because there is absolutely no way that should have been given as six. The biggest game in cricket, watched by millions of people all over the world, and they got the rules wrong. How can that happen? There weren't just two umpires, there was a third and a fourth umpire watching it upstairs. And none of them knew that it should have been five runs instead of six. I didn't know the rule either, but I was a fan sat in the crowd! The Kiwis took it well, as they had to, but I bet they were seething inside. Had any of those four umpires known the rules, they would have won their first World Cup, not England.

After winning the World Cup, England's players should have been everywhere and lionised as heroes. The England and Wales Cricket Board (ECB) and players' agents should have been working overtime, trying to get those players all over the radio, on chat shows, panel shows, *Question Time*, *Newsnight* and *Saturday Superstore*, in the papers, on websites, pretty much anywhere that would have them, for their own benefit and the benefit of English cricket. But English cricket is terrible at marketing itself and its players. When I was playing, one of the ECB's big things was wanting players to be recognised by at least 10 per cent of the population. That doesn't sound like many people, but it's actually a very ambitious number. We had a meeting about it, and when I asked how they were going to achieve it, they replied, 'We just want you to be recognised.'

'But how are we going to make that happen? What are we going to do?'

'We hadn't really thought about that. We'd just like you to be.'

They didn't have a plan of action, it was just some woolly notion. It seemed that nothing changed much after I retired, which meant that the World Cup victory, which was shown on terrestrial TV and watched by millions in the UK, wasn't capitalised on. I know from working in TV that producers, commissioners and the like aren't interested in having cricketers on shows because they don't sell. They don't usually play on terrestrial TV, the public don't know who they are, so TV people aren't interested in them either. So England winning the World Cup was the perfect time to get players out there, promoting themselves and the game. But it didn't happen, the euphoria quickly died down, and how many of those England players would be recognised if they walked into a pub today? Probably Ben, but that's about it.

Then again, I remember doing a Morrisons advert just after retiring and getting recognised more than I ever did playing cricket. I think they must have been showing it a lot during *X Factor* breaks. That made me realise how small the world of cricket is. Now, there are people who watch me on various things who don't even know I played cricket, like I used to watch Andrew Castle present GMTV and have no idea he played tennis.

CHAPTER FIVE

YOU'RE CANCELLED

Usually when people say something is 'political correctness gone mad', what they really mean is they're upset that someone has been called out for saying something racist, homophobic or sexist. So political correctness is a good thing. It basically means having respect for other people, not saying things that might upset people, make them feel uncomfortable or excluded. But – and I'm about to contradict myself slightly – it has got slightly out of hand.

Now, people are constantly being hammered for accidentally saying the 'wrong' thing. It might not even be racist, homophobic or sexist, it might just be a word or an opinion that was perfectly acceptable last week but has suddenly become problematic. There are also people policing what people are and aren't talking about, or whose social-media posts they're liking or retweeting. Sometimes it's difficult to know what you're allowed to have an opinion on, how to say it and whether you should open your mouth at all.

It used to be easy to spot if people were being nasty or rude. And if you saw someone being nasty or rude, you'd do something about it. Or would you? Recently, I watched a drama series called *The Loudest Voice* about Roger Ailes, the former chairman of Fox News, who was a serial sexual abuser. I found myself wincing a lot and thinking, 'I've never come across anyone like this. How is it allowed to happen? Why didn't anyone stop him?' It's tempting to think that had you been there, you would have said something. But clearly it's not as simple as that. The horrible truth is that had I been around 40 or 50 years ago, I probably would have been a complete dinosaur by modern standards. You see clips of old sitcoms now, like *Love Thy Neighbour* (which is about a white couple who live next door to a black couple) and can't believe it ever got made, because it's just so racist. They made eight series, so obviously it was a big hit in the ratings.

The difference now is that people who have genuinely made mistakes are being hammered. Their crime might be making a point too clumsily or using the wrong terminology. That doesn't necessarily mean they're prejudiced or discriminatory, it might just mean they didn't get the memo. Take people identifying as someone or something else. If someone wants to be a dog or whatever they want to be, I'm not bothered. That's their business. But if I forget that they think they're a dog, don't get your knickers in a twist about it. I just forgot! And no doubt if I use the phrase 'don't get your knickers in a twist', someone will pop up and tell me that that's a horribly sexist phrase, which perpetuates the stereotype that women are more likely to get hysterical. That just shows you how ridiculous it is, because I thought men were allowed to wear knickers anyway? People are so intolerant, unforgiving and spiteful. That's why we've got this cancel culture, because people love getting offended and jumping on people's mistakes or opinions that vary from theirs. It's a national sport.

That's why I'm better off away from social media, because I can't keep up with the terminology. I'm a bloke from Preston, end of story. The idea of identifying as something or someone else means nothing to me. It makes no sense. If someone else wants to identify as something or someone else, that's fine by me. I'll be polite and go along with it. But it's like *Catchphrase*, 'say what you see', in that I might get it wrong. I'd sincerely apologise for that, but I wouldn't mean anything by it. I won't do it on purpose or mean to hurt anyone, I'll just have made a mistake. Not everyone has to understand each other, as long as people respect each other. There are people out there saying all sorts of stuff that's quite obviously horrible and nasty, on purpose, so have a go at them instead!

The closest I've come to being 'cancelled' was when I was on social media a few years ago and having a bit of back and forth with Jimmy Anderson about Preston and Burnley, which is where he comes from. I said something about people from Burnley having a special six-finger handshake and the town crier having to read out his tweets, all of it in good humour, and people started having a go at me for being prejudiced against under-privileged people and people with disabilities. Of course I wasn't, but I've learned that the excuse that you were just having a laugh and a joke with a mate doesn't wash with some people. Then there was an interview I did with

Piers Morgan for *GQ* magazine. I told him a story about being in a hotel, phoning reception and the woman not being able to understand my food order, because of my thick Preston accent and the fact she wasn't originally from England. The media picked up on it and suddenly I was a racist, the second coming of Enoch Powell. The *Daily Mail* headline was, 'Andrew Flintoff in bizarre anti-immigration outburst.' I thought, 'Do I really have to explain this?', before ignoring it and letting it go away. You could drive yourself mad trying to analyse if what people are saying about you has any merit, but I knew I hadn't said anything wrong. And they wonder why so many sportspeople don't give interviews, or if they do, they sound so vanilla. Why would you bother if saying something innocuous can get you into hot water? It's got to the stage where there are opinions I hold that I'd never make public, for fear of never working again.

When I used to play for England in South Africa, they had a quota system, which meant that they had to pick X number of black players. That could be a little bit frustrating from a competitive point of view, because it meant we weren't playing against their best possible team. But when I think about it now, it made sense. Making sure black people got opportunities that had been denied to them for so long was more important than the outcome of a game of cricket. For the same reason, maybe a woman getting a presenting job is more important, in terms of changing the overall culture, than a bloke missing out on a job that he should have got according to his credentials.

In the meantime, there will be disgruntled people on both sides, like we're seeing now with sports punditry. There are still people who have a problem with female pundits in men's sport, whether it be football, cricket or rugby union. The argument goes that they can't possibly know what they're talking about because they haven't played it. But someone like Alex Scott is amazing, she clearly knows what she's talking about. And she's miles better than some of the men. They've all played men's football to a high level, but they're not very good at articulating their knowledge. It's the same in cricket. I listen to them sometimes and think, 'What are you on?' It's like they never played the game. Playing at the highest level isn't everything.

And I don't understand the problem with female sports presenters at all. Laura Woods on talkSPORT is brilliant at what she does.

In some ways it's a good thing that people are more open about what offends them, because it means that people take more care over what they say and maybe we live in a kinder society. I popped into the England dressing room not so long ago and it seemed very different to my day, a far nicer place. Twenty years ago, any chink in your armour and people would be all over you. Because I was overweight, I got slaughtered. I couldn't say anything, I just had to own the jokes and take the piss out of myself, however much it hurt me inside. Doing that meant I had some semblance of control. It was a very different world 20 years ago, people said far harsher stuff than they do now.

I also got a terrible kicking in the press for being fat, and walking out for one game between England and Zimbabwe at Old Trafford was one of the worst feelings ever. I was overcome with this feeling of self-loathing and shame. Because it was cricket, I couldn't even run away, I just had to stand there for hours getting abuse from the crowd. And while I was eventually able to manage the abuse, I never really came to terms with it. It was a lonely place for a long time and opened up wounds that will probably never heal.

But while it's good that racism, homophobia and things like fat-shaming are now frowned upon, and that certain environments are less ruthless and more welcoming, it would be a very bland world if piss-taking was outlawed completely. If my mates stopped taking the piss out of me for being slightly ginger, having a big mole in the middle of my head or having a belly I can never get rid of, I'd be slightly worried. Because in my circle of friends, having the piss taken out of you has nothing to do with nastiness, it's a test of how strong the bonds of friendship are and means you're accepted.

I don't mind having a laugh about my mental health. I realise my behaviour is a bit irrational at times and my mates take the piss out of me for it. For me, that's a way of getting through it. I'm not saying it works for everyone, but if I don't mind people taking the piss out of my irrational behaviour, and it actually helps me deal with it, that should be the end of it.

I'm never going to be an advocate of the 'pull yourself together and man up' school of snapping someone out of depression. But I sometimes have to do a bit of that to myself. I'll give myself a talking to and tell myself to buck up. The way I see it, if you're not willing to put any effort in, it's difficult for anyone else to help. But not everyone is like me. Some people talk about their depression a lot. But that could be a form of therapy in itself, and if it makes them feel better about themselves, I can't really criticise them. But others like to point the finger and claim that certain people aren't 'doing depression' the right way. That's not fair, because who knows what's going on in people's heads and everyone has different ways of coping with things.

Sometimes, it's hard to know the 'correct' way of behaving. The truth is, there is no correct way. It's lovely that a lot more people now are understanding and sympathetic, but that approach isn't for everyone. I'm not hanging around with lads who cuddle each other and tell each other they're brilliant all the time. That's not for me. And I find a lot of it is false. I'm always hearing people say 'be kind' nowadays, as if it's some kind of deep philosophical directive. But just because someone is going around telling everyone else to 'be kind', that doesn't necessarily make them kind. It's similar to people who say 'be humble'. Often, they need to take their own advice.

I'm not sure kids are growing up soft but I worry that they have a very low tolerance to certain things. I know everyone wants the world to be a lovely place, but it's really not. There's always going to be people who think differently to you, you're always going to be competing for things and sometimes it's going to be ugly and unpleasant. That's why schools that don't believe in competition are letting kids down because they're not preparing them for reality. They don't pick the best people for their teams in the name of inclusivity, but that's not how the real world is.

In the real world, the people who work the hardest get the jobs. Now, kids are entering the workplace and expecting to be handed things on a plate, because that's what they've been taught will happen. Well, that can't happen, because the older people in the company probably worked bloody hard to get where they have. What do they think their boss is going to say?

'Right, so you'd like a promotion, but you've only been here six months and don't really know anything yet? Fine, you can have Trevor's job, he's probably been here too long now and knows too much.'

That's why I'm tough on my boys when it comes to their cricket. So many people play sport, so you've got to be bloody good at it if you want to turn it into a career. People think sport is romantic, and it can be. But it's just so bloody cut-throat and not always the healthiest environment.

They need to learn that no one is going to give them anything, they are going to have to fight tooth and claw for everything they get. They have to learn that there will always be rivals trying to get one over them. That being the case, you have to be prepared to crawl over broken glass to get one over them. That applies to every sportsperson, even the likes of Michael Jordan and Lionel Messi. Yes, they're extremely talented, but they might never have made it if they hadn't been ruthless and worked like dogs. I think giving kids tough home truths is better than pretending that everything and everyone will be lovely.

Too many people are too self-righteous nowadays. They think that because they find something offensive, everyone should find it offensive – and whoever doesn't find it offensive is guilty by association. But there aren't many things that someone, somewhere, won't find offensive, so people are always having to watch what they say. Apart from Piers Morgan, who says what he thinks, usually backed up by facts, which is why so many people dislike him.

Some people want to create their own truth, believe what they want to believe, and deny any facts that don't fit their narrative or ideology. Even if you show them actual scientific facts, they'll say they're wrong and start getting abusive. When did this start, this denial of scientific facts? And when did people start bullying people who believed in scientific facts? It's so weird.

Anyone being abused for what they look like is horrible. I know, because I had a taste of it. And I'm all for body confidence and people feeling comfortable in their own skin. That's something that everyone should aim for. But we shouldn't allow the waters to get clouded. We now have a situation where fat activists are claiming that there's nothing wrong with being obese, and that anyone who points out that being obese isn't great for you is bigoted. That's just ridiculous. There's a difference between fat-shaming and stating facts, and it's scientific fact that being obese is bad for your health. It increases the chances of you getting all sorts of diseases and anyone who thinks otherwise is deluded.

Nowadays, everyone's got an opinion on everything and isn't afraid to shout about it from the rooftops. Or, as we call the rooftops in this day and age, social media. Everyone knows how to play football better than actual professional footballers, everyone knows science better than actual scientists, everyone knew how to run the country during the coronavirus lockdown, everyone knew what the long-term implications of coronavirus would be. There was a time when people went to university or learned a trade and could then claim to be an expert in something. But now, everyone thinks they know everything because they've got a Twitter account. And they can't handle being told what to do, because they think they already know the answers.

My head doesn't work like that. When there's a discussion going on, I'll often go really quiet, either because I'm desperately trying to think of something to add to the conversation or I simply don't give a shit. Or, if I'm in the mood, I'll say exactly what's in my head, which sometimes doesn't go down very well. I try to keep it short and as honest as possible, but I can tell you from experience that it doesn't normally go down very well, because people don't like opinions that are different to theirs. Other times, a topic will come up that I genuinely know quite a bit about. Maybe it will be cricket, which I obviously know inside out. And I'll be sat there listening to a conversation thinking, 'Everyone's talking absolute bollocks. People are actually making things up.' And it's usually the people who are talking bollocks and making things up that are telling other people they're wrong. But I can't be arsed saying anything. Except maybe when they leave, when I tell everyone they were full of shit.

I've had plenty of dads tell me about cricket, including about games I played in. I've had people tell me how *A League of Their Own* works, or how it should work. I've had people tell me stories about colleagues on various shows and what they're 'really' like. I just try not to engage, mainly because it's madness people telling me about my own life but also because that would mean having a longer conversation. Now I'm doing *Top Gear*, almost every bloke I meet has an opinion on it. People will start talking to me about how much they loved or hated Clarkson or how good or bad Matt LeBlanc was. And everyone wants to know what the best car is. My answer is always the same, and quite disappointing for some people: if you like a car, you like a car. Whatever your budget is, get the nicest car you can afford. Unless you're a car geek, modern cars pretty much all drive the same. But that doesn't stop people saying things like, 'You say that, but from third to fourth, the BMW X5 is an absolute dream. But the differential on an Audi A6 is in a different class completely …' Sometimes I'll think, 'Turn it off, will you?' But other times I'll spout the biggest load of bollocks you've ever heard, while laughing inside.

While I do think that people are more likely to be offended nowadays, that's not to say people didn't used to get offended. The main difference is that people weren't allowed to say they were offended and put up with it in silence, which is maybe even worse. I think that we now have a situation where people – especially younger people – are more sensitive, combined with the fact that there are more ways of being offended. Someone can offend you to your face, over the phone, via email, text or WhatsApp, on Twitter, Instagram, Facebook or TikTok. It doesn't help that some people, including me, aren't very good at expressing themselves online, which makes for misunderstandings. But on top of that, people have realised that they can use being offended – or pretending to be offended – to their advantage. By kicking up a stink, they can make people feel bad, get people to dance to their tune and stay relevant.

As I've got older, I've developed this thing whereby I mutter stuff under my breath if someone is talking bollocks, probably because I'm getting less tolerant of other people's nonsense. My kids have picked up on it, so they'll say, 'Talking to yourself again, Dad?' And my standard reply is, 'Yes, it's the only way I can have a sensible conversation around here.' But sometimes if I disagree with something, the muttering will come out a bit loud and get me into trouble. It's not quite Tourette's, but it's similar. If I'm talking to someone and they're not paying attention, I'll suddenly blurt out, 'You're not even fucking listening!'

When I'm in meetings now, I'll say exactly what I think, because I think giving an honest opinion is the right thing to do. But I had one recently which I thought went really well, in which I thought I'd given lots of constructive input from a good place, and afterwards my agent Katie started shaking her head and said, 'What was that? I was cringing all the way through.' I replied, 'Oh, really? To be honest, I thought it went really well.' I was certainly getting it all wrong in my head. I've never really been tactful, but I think I'm getting worse. It's like my filter has gone faulty and stuff is getting through that didn't used to. And once it's out, you obviously can't put it back in. The deed has been done. And in these politically correct times, when saying what you really think can have terrible consequences, lacking tact can be dangerous.

Part of me can't wait to get old, because old people don't give a shit who they offend. Not long after our new baby was born, I took him to see my grandpa, along with a pie. We walked into his flat and my grandpa said, 'I'm not feeling well, put the pie in the kitchen and go if you want.' I said, 'I've driven an hour to be here.' And he replied, 'Nah, you get off.' I was there for about three minutes, but I thought, 'Fair play, he doesn't want us there.' People might think that's a bit weird, but I wasn't offended. Why would you be? He didn't want us round his house, that was the end of it. That's one of the fun things about getting older, you're allowed to say exactly what you think and people aren't really allowed to be offended. That said, I don't really want to wait until I'm 92 to be able to say what I want. And anyway, the rules for old people might have changed by then and perhaps it will acceptable to shout at them for saying the 'wrong' thing, just like anyone else.

CHAPTER SIX

LOCKDOWN LOWDOWN

The world will never be the same after coronavirus. America certainly hasn't come out of it too well. They've got millions of middle-class people on food parcels, a health system that can't cope and a load of nutters who think the whole thing was a hoax. Sometimes I think America must be having a massive nervous breakdown.

I find Donald Trump compulsive viewing. Guilty pleasures are usually things like *Love Island* or the Spice Girls, but my biggest is the leader of the free world. He's so unhinged he's clearly a massive danger to his own people and the rest of the world, so the fact that he amuses me so much is probably quite wrong. I'd tune into CNN every night to watch him doing his daily briefing and it would be like a dark comedy sketch. Whenever he spoke, you could tell when he was on script, because he'd almost be talking like a normal human being. But you could see his advisers hovering over his shoulder, looking tense. Not because he was talking about really important things, like the fact that thousands more Americans had died that day, but because they were terrified of what he might say. You could almost see them thinking, 'That's it, Donald, just keep reading the words on the page ...' And then he'd spread his arms and start looking around the room, and you knew he was going to say something weird. Like suggesting that people should inject bleach or announcing that he'd been sucking Strepsils to ward off infection. He ended up telling people to take some anti-malarial drug that doctors had to point out might increase the chances of dying from coronavirus. Even then, he wouldn't stop: 'It's fine, I'm taking it. Go on, take it! It will do you the world of good ...'

Watching Trump is like watching a parody. He's like the longest-running *Saturday Night Live* sketch in history. I'm a 42-year-old bloke who was educated at an average school and have no qualifications apart from a few GCSEs, yet every time Trump opens his mouth I think, 'That can't be right.' When he starts freestyling is usually when he gets himself into trouble. But he only gets himself into trouble with some people, because he says things with such conviction that his own people believe him. The way he carries on reminds me of when I was a kid and you'd have mates who would march up to a queue outside a nightclub and brazenly salute the bouncers. Sometimes it would work and the bouncers would smile back and wave them in.

Everyone says Donald Trump is thick, but he can't be thick. I know he inherited a load of money from his dad and has lost loads of money, but he's still a multi-billionaire with loads of businesses. I've been to his hotel in Scotland and it's beautiful. And he became president of the United States! If you're able to convince tens of millions of the public to vote for you as their leader, you can't possibly be thick. Then again, we're talking about a country where more than a third of the population don't believe in evolution and almost half of Republicans polled thought Bill Gates would use coronavirus vaccines to implant microchips. I want to believe Trump is chucking new stuff out there every day to throw the media off the scent, so that he can focus on the serious business of managing the country.

You watch CNN and they don't even try to hide their disdain for him. But I think the fact they're constantly bagging on him works in his favour, because it makes people feel sympathetic towards him. They watch all these very clever, smug journalists and anchors making smart remarks and think they're picking on their man, especially those who are naturally inclined to vote Republican.

But maybe I'm giving Donald Trump too much credit. I suspect he's actually a conman and a psychopath who's so far out of his depth it's terrifying, and that there are a load of competent people running around in the background covering his arse and keeping things going. But however bad Donald Trump is and whatever is going on behind the scenes, imagine how bad the Democrats must be. If I was Hillary Clinton, I'd spend a lot of time looking at myself in the mirror and thinking, 'How shit must I be if I couldn't beat that lad?' How many people have accused him of sexual assault? Almost 20? And that's in the age of the Me Too movement. He's had hundreds of lawsuits filed against him, loads of associates convicted of crimes and he still might get in next time, because all the

Democrats can come up with as an opponent is a 77-year-old man with a habit of putting his foot in it.

I think Trump panics, opens his mouth and stuff comes out that he had no idea was even inside his head. Then after he's spouted bollocks for 20 minutes, his health officials, poor old Dr Fauci and Dr Birx, have to follow him on stage, contradict him without making it too obvious, and somehow tie everything up and make it look as if everyone's on the same page. When I was on talkSPORT, Ally McCoist and Laura Woods would some-times have to be my Dr Fauci and Dr Birx respectively.

I'm torn when it comes to America. I love going there, it's an amazing place. And I love Americans, although they are annoying. They're such positive people, they genuinely want everything to be great and everyone to be having a good time. But they wind me up at the same time. Corona-virus seems to have magnified all their problems, including the inequality and rampant individualism. While every other developed country was in lockdown, they were carrying on as normal. It was bonkers. People were screaming and shouting because they couldn't get a haircut or a massage. Who needs a massage that much? Just get your wife or husband to give you one. Then there were the tattoo people. Seriously, who needs a tattoo during a pandemic? As in, actually needs one? I must admit, I was planning to get some tattoos before coronavirus came along. But once lockdown kicked in and all the ink parlours closed, I didn't take to the streets with a placard that read, 'IT IS MY HUMAN RIGHT TO GET A TATTOO! STOP THE TYRANNY!'

In America's defence, there are a lot of people in that country – something like 330 million – so it's only natural that there are a lot of idiots. And these idiots, who keep turning up on the telly shouting about their right to a manicure or a foot rub, make all Americans look like complete dickheads. In my opinion, their constitution needs ripping up because these idiots are always using it and its various amendments to justify their actions, whether it's the right to be homophobic or racist or wandering around with machine guns.

Meanwhile, back in leafy Cheshire, I thought I was being very naughty by popping out to the supermarket. As I was driving over there, my heart would skip a beat whenever

I saw a police car. And then I'd switch on the telly and see some American woman having a meltdown in a supermarket because someone had told her to put a mask on, or a load of college kids packed into a swimming pool in Florida, drinking cocktails and snogging each other. Some people in America honestly thought the whole thing was a conspiracy theory. As you know, I like a conspiracy theory. But we are entering a whole new world of madness where people think someone has made up a virus when tens of thousands of fellow Americans are dying of it and the hospitals are full to bursting point. I can only assume they thought the media was making everything up. You've got no chance with people like that, they're a lost cause. The level of stupidity is so completely off the scale, I'm not sure they should be allowed to leave the house, let alone vote in elections.

I hope that the main lesson we learn from coronavirus is how important certain people's roles are for society. Before coronavirus came along, we had the government referring to NHS workers as 'low-skilled'. Low-skilled? They're saving the world! While most people, including sportspeople and pointless celebrities, were sat at home watching Netflix and making videos of themselves doing press-ups or washing their hands, these so-called low-skilled NHS workers were risking their lives to treat patients struck down with coronavirus. And it was the same with carers and bus drivers and delivery drivers and all sorts of other people who don't earn much money. It showed how topsy-turvy society is, that the people needed to keep society functioning during a deadly pandemic are paid peanuts in comparison, while people whose jobs don't benefit society in the slightest are on bundles of money. If you were to view society as a house, those key workers would be the foundations, floors, walls and roofs – easily forgotten, but absolutely vital to structural integrity. And inside the house, celebrities and footballers and the like would be giant TVs and ludicrously expensive kitchen units – nice to look at but expendable.

I found the Thursday night clapping a little bit awkward, because the houses on our road are quite spread out and it was just us on the doorstep and the distant sound of others doing the same, in that very polite English fashion. You could tell people wanted to cheer and shout but they were too English to really show how appreciative they were. But it was also quite moving. I'm not a very emotional person but I'd watch or read a story about doctors and nurses putting their lives at risks to save others and find myself welling up a little bit. That sort of heroism blows my mind and makes me feel quite insignificant by comparison. It's the closest thing most of us will see to soldiers going off to war to fight on our behalf and I can't even begin to comprehend what they went through. God knows how they felt when they saw pictures of people having picnics and barbecues in the park when they were supposed to be indoors, but I hope that those clapping sessions made them feel a little bit more appreciated.

I think there's been a big shift in terms of how people view who is and who isn't vital for society. But while clapping is nice, I hope there will be correction in terms of how much they're paid. That would happen in a fair, sane society. But I'm not holding my breath. I suspect that as soon as everything is back to normal again, whenever that is and whatever normal will look like, everyone will have a big party, get smashed, wake up the next morning and think, 'Bloody hell, that coronavirus was hard work. But might as well crack on.' People will thank their lucky stars they're not nurses or carers, those key workers will be forgotten about again and some people will be even hungrier to earn their next million. While some idealistic people will say that coronavirus will make people rethink the importance of money, I think it might have the opposite effect.

I get the argument that coronavirus has shown that health is more important than money, but real life is a lot more complicated than that. The importance of having money became abundantly clear during the pandemic, because without money, it was a lot harder to ride it out. People with decent jobs were able to take a pay cut for a few months and still pay their bills, but that wasn't the case for poorer people. And look at America, where for a lot of relatively wealthy people, losing their job meant losing their health care.

The government, which has been finding money from everywhere, will have to tighten its belt, and we know who loses out when governments tighten belts.

It shows how messed up society's priorities are. Sport's nice and being without it during the pandemic left a big void in a lot of people's lives, but it doesn't matter. Not really.

I understood people's frustrations, but there were bigger things at stake than whether the football, cricket or rugby seasons should be completed, namely people getting seriously ill and dying. It wouldn't have bothered me in the slightest if the Premier League season had been cancelled and Liverpool had not won the title (although I wouldn't have stood in the middle of Liverpool and shouted that). The Olympics don't really matter, Wimbledon doesn't really matter, even cricket doesn't really matter.

Coronavirus certainly made me question my usefulness. When I was growing up and wanting to play cricket for Lancashire and England, it seemed like the most important thing in the world. It was all I wanted to do, so it had to be important. Surely? And when I started making decent money and people were giving me adulation, it seemed to make even more sense that I was doing something important. It's the same with the stuff I've done in TV. But none of what I've done has been important in the grand scheme of things, apart from maybe my documentaries. If I hadn't played cricket for England, someone else would have played instead. If I hadn't been a team captain on *A League of Their Own*, someone else would have been. And if I hadn't presented *Top Gear*, someone else would have presented it. The world wouldn't have been any different. People wouldn't have even noticed. So I can only conclude that I'm completely pointless.

I've got God knows how many followers on Twitter but when the world was in meltdown, people needed saving and useful people were running around plugging all the leaks, where was I? Sat at home looking at trainers on the internet, because a man who can bat, bowl and talk about cars isn't much use during a global crisis. And I think a lot of people would have had the same thought during the pandemic. What's the point of the job I do if I can be mothballed for months and no one really notices? It's quite sobering and I wonder whether there will be an upsurge of people quitting their old, pointless jobs and training to do jobs that really benefit society. Then again, probably not. Look what happened when they appealed for fruit pickers, hardly anyone signed up. They had to fly Romanians in, because British people were content to sit around doing nowt.

Personally, the fact that there was no cricket for most of the summer was a blessing in disguise. Me and the boys practised a bit at home but I wasn't taking them here, there and everywhere like normal. Too much sport can throw a family apart, so the lockdown was a good thing in a way, because it brought us closer together. It was important to try and take some positives from a bad situation, and I was made for lockdown anyway. I've probably been isolating for years and not even known it. I don't really need to be around people and don't do much when I'm not working. I'm perfectly happy in my own company for days on end and if I've got my family around me, that'll do me. It also made me acutely aware of what I really need in my life, materially. If you took everything out of my house that I didn't need, I'd probably be left with a bed and a couch. That's about it. Oh, and my trainer collection.

Getting to spend some time at home was great, especially because I got to spend time with the new baby. I'd get up late, throw on a T-shirt and bum around all day. Then when I landed a job presenting talkSPORT's Breakfast show, I'd roll out of bed at 5.30 a.m., have a quick shower, make myself look half-decent, do the show and go back to bed. I didn't have to worry about getting on a plane and jetting off somewhere or sitting in a hotel in a strange city, looking forward to getting home and seeing everyone again.

Work–life balance is something I'm always striving to get right. Playing professional cricket is not great for relationships or family life, but at least you know where you're going to be most of the time. With what I do now, it's feast or famine. You can be sat at home for a couple of weeks thinking, 'This is nice, I could get used to this.' Then suddenly you're constantly checking your phone, wondering why your agent hasn't been in touch. Or some work will crop up and you'll suddenly have to wrap your head around the fact that you'll be away from home for God knows how long.

I sometimes wonder how I keep getting offered work. It confuses me. And I'm constantly wrestling with whether I should take the work or not. Whatever the offer is, part of me thinks, 'No, don't take this one. Have a bit of time off.' But there's always the fear that if you do reject it, nothing will come up again for months. Or maybe ever again. Then there's the money. I'm essentially a working-class lad, so I know what it's like not having very much. But I also feel a bit guilty, because I remember how hard my dad had to work to earn his wages. I'll think, 'They're paying me how much to do what?' And then I'll think, 'Well, in that case, I should probably go and do it.' But after being away for a week or so I'll start missing the kids and know I'm not getting the balance right. Thankfully, the kids understand and just get on with it. And if I was one of those dads that gets up at six every morning, puts on a suit and doesn't get home until seven in the evening, they'd probably spend less time with me anyway than if I was doing what I do, which is lots of interesting things.

During lockdown, the kids were all schooled remotely of course. They were all in the annexe and at their desks at 9 a.m. on the dot and didn't finish until 3.45 p.m., like a proper school day. They even got their normal break times, an hour and a half for lunch and games lessons, with me as the teacher. I was surprised at how disciplined they were; they got their heads down, cracked on with their work and I didn't hear a peep out of them most days. There was no chance of them wandering in while I was in the middle of doing the radio show, which seemed to be happening all over the place during lockdown.

Not that I did any teaching in the classroom, because I'm absolutely useless. Anything I did learn at school I've long since forgotten. My daughter was 15, so there was no chance of me being able to help her in any way. And my oldest son was 14, which isn't much different. I might have had some clue what my 12-year-old was learning, but only if I'd pushed myself. All the teaching was done online, which made me wonder what would have happened had a pandemic struck pre-internet. Not a lot, I suspect. The only problem came when they were supposed to break up for Easter and I decided to change the term times. That didn't go down too well. But when I did finally let them out, rather than going all *Lord of the Flies* on me, they pretty much ignored their phones and iPads and spent most of their time playing outside. I put a cricket net up on the path leading out of the garage, did a bit of coaching with the boys and it was really quite idyllic.

Lockdown was frustrating in some ways, but most of those frustrations were trivial. Before I went in the jungle for *I'm a Celebrity*, someone told me that people adapt to those kinds of situations in different ways. Some people get freaked out by it and struggle to adapt, some people rebel against it and start acting up and some people accept it quite quickly, so that a weird situation soon becomes the norm. And just as in the jungle, as soon as I closed the doors of the house, I just got on with things. My wife also put together 20,000 care packages for Manchester hospitals.

I had to isolate for a week before lockdown proper, because I'd just got back from Australia. That was difficult, because it's the most natural thing in the world to walk through the door after being away for a few weeks and give everyone a cuddle. I spent most of my isolation in a bedroom on the top floor, despite not having any symptoms. And even though I knew I could have it despite not having any symptoms, and give it to other people, it still didn't feel right. Not only could I not touch anyone, I couldn't be within two metres of anyone. I was like Jane Eyre's madwoman in the attic, imprisoned in my own house. Or the Invisible Man. I could see everything going on around me but couldn't interact with anything. I wasn't even allowed to touch inanimate objects, and almost as soon as my clothes came off, my missus was carrying on as if they had to be incinerated. Maybe they were?

My parents are both over 70, so I was obviously worried about their health. They also weren't able to see the baby, which was hard for them. On top of that, the kids got bored and missed their friends at times, and it's challenging living in close proximity to anyone for that long. But not having some things in your kitchen cupboards that you usually do, or not being able to get toilet paper, or have the dessert you wanted with your dinner, or the right shape of pasta, or the right cut of steak, isn't the end of the world. Just wipe your arse with a newspaper and eat something different. It's not like we were cowering in a shelter every night, listening to bombs being dropped. Instead, we were sitting in a living room, eating beans on toast and watching *Tiger King* on

Netflix. I realise that lockdown must have been a lot harder than that for a lot of people, but we kind of managed to make it work. I'd been working quite hard before lockdown, doing a lot of travelling with *Top Gear*, so I just viewed it as taking a bit of time off, spending precious time with the family and gaining a new perspective on what was and wasn't important in life. I hope other people will have done the same and concluded that some of the things they thought were important were of no importance at all, and some of the things they'd perhaps neglected were actually crucial. Having given it a lot of thought myself, there isn't much that is important apart from my family and friends.

When I saw what was going on in the supermarkets just before lockdown kicked in, I couldn't believe it. People literally fighting over bags of rice and potatoes. It just showed how incredibly spoilt and entitled some people are. Suddenly, people were going out of their minds because they didn't have any Diet Cokes or broccoli in the larder. Sometimes, I think that humankind is going backwards rather than advancing. That can be the only explanation for people being told that a disease has arrived that will kill millions of people and their first reaction being, 'Shit, but what are we going to do about bog roll?'

Another thing that happened during lockdown was that everyone became an expert in pandemics. While I was only venturing out a couple of times a day for exercise and basic provisions, and spending the rest of the time hunkered down in my house and listening to the advice of actual medical experts, other people were treating the world to their views on coronavirus. Instead of taking advantage of time off from work to learn to play a musical instrument, it was as if half the country had done crash-course PhDs in virology. I had thought it was just football managers who didn't know what they were talking about, but it turns out that medical professionals who have spent decades studying infectious diseases don't know anything either. Had the pubs still been open, no doubt there would have been middle-aged men sat around tables slagging off various doctors, instead of players in their team.

And people haven't just become overnight experts in pandemics, everyone suddenly became a personal trainer.

I did a couple of Instagram Lives with my mate Stan, who's an actual PT. But I didn't take the class, Stan did, I was just helping him out. But every man and his dog (sometimes literally) was suddenly doing PT instruction. Tyson Fury, who's one of my guilty pleasures, was the only one worth watching. He was on every morning at nine o'clock and it was lots of fun. His kids kept running in the room, he had to keep telling them to get out and it made me love him even more. How much money has Tyson Fury got? Tens of millions of pounds? And he's living in a house on Morecambe Bay and doing exercise routines every morning, which is brilliant.

I suppose everyone was just trying to find something to do that was relevant to the situation. That's why we had so many celebrities doing funny skits, dancing in their kitchens and singing songs in their gardens. Because they had a captive audience, they knew that they could throw any old shit out there and millions of people would watch it. That was them saying, 'Look at me! Look at me! I'm still here!' I'm sure some of them thought they were saving the world, one tweet at a time. I think others just saw it as an opportunity. There's something a bit odd about battling for likes during a global pandemic and the competition to get the biggest names on Instagram Live was quite unseemly. There were even people subtly but not subtly pushing their endorsement deals, doing press-up challenges with products lying about. The worst thing about it was that I'd find myself watching them, so that I spent far too long in lockdown feeling disappointed in myself.

I'm always fighting technology to some extent, and don't really understand the point of using your phone to turn the heating or lights on. What's wrong with switches on the wall? Is it seriously too much effort to raise your arm to just above shoulder height and press a button with your finger? I preferred it when phones were phones. When the Queen gave a speech during lockdown, one of my lads spotted the big old-fashioned phone on her desk and said, 'Why has she got such a bad phone when she's got all that money?' And I replied, 'Because the Queen understands that a phone is for calling people on, nothing else.'

I remember getting my first mobile phone when I was about 17, taking it home and my dad saying, 'They're rubbish, them, they'll never catch on.' I honestly wish he'd been right. In fact, I'll go one step further and say I wish they'd never been invented. I hate the fact that someone can get to you at any moment (I hide my phone around the house, so that I don't know it's ringing, because I really need to psyche myself up for a phone call). But if I don't answer, someone will phone my missus to get to me instead, as I have a phobia of phones.

But technology certainly came into its own during lockdown. As well as the kids being taught remotely, their grandparents were able to see them whenever they wanted on FaceTime. Having said that, there was a downside. There's always a downside. Suddenly, I was in hundreds of WhatsApp groups. It started with one, and then someone in that group put me in another one, and someone in that group put me in another one, and eventually half of England seemed to have my number. I'd wake up every morning to 200 messages. It was an absolute nightmare. I'd think, 'I can't be arsed with this. Why is everyone suddenly speaking to each other? Why have they waited until a global pandemic?' And because people can see if you've read their message or not, people know you're ignoring them, which obviously isn't a great look.

Meanwhile, people were getting arsy with me because I hadn't commented on some dirty picture they'd sent. Mind you, that's no different to normal. I've been on one group chat for years and never said anything. I haven't got the heart or courage to leave. Seriously, if anyone's got a problem, let me know – but I don't sit around texting, ringing and Face-Timing people in normal times. They literally had nothing to talk about apart from coronavirus and what they were having for dinner.

I also kept getting invites to Houseparty. The kids had been using Houseparty before lockdown, to chat with their friends, and I was constantly telling them to get off it, because as far as I was concerned, it was just kids looking at a screen. And suddenly all my mates were saying, 'Get yourself on Houseparty and we can all have a chat.' And I was thinking, 'I've spent the last six months telling my kids to get off Houseparty, I can't be normalising it.' Whoever owns Houseparty and Zoom must have been raking it in. I turned up at one of these Houseparties and didn't know who was there. I was looking at all these phone numbers with international dialling codes and I didn't recognise any of them. It was like when you turn up to a real house party and you're shouldering past a load of strangers in the hallway, terrified that you won't find anyone you know. And just as you're about to turn around and leave, someone shouts at you from the kitchen. And you think, 'Oh shit, he's seen me ...' Apparently, the same groups of people were on Houseparty and Zoom every week, while eating dinner and drinking shit loads of booze. It's almost as if chatting to people was a new craze. People were suddenly having weekly chats with old mates they hadn't contacted for years. I even found myself caught up in this new fad. I'd find myself having conversations about politics or shopping or the lack of kale in Waitrose, or coming across as rude by not saying anything (I found that a good trick was to not move for ages and pretend your screen had frozen). Then the Houseparty would finish and I'd vow never to do it again, before finding myself on another one a week later.

People were always going to be upset about the dickheads not obeying isolation and social-distancing guidelines, but the real miracle was that tens of millions of people obeyed the rules for so long. I didn't drive for weeks and when I did take the car out for the first time, I really had to fight the temptation to cut loose, because I was champing at the bit and the roads were almost empty. There were more pushbikes on the roads than cars, and the only people on the pavements were joggers. People were pedalling up hills and pounding the streets who had never cycled or run anywhere in their lives, all because they'd been told they couldn't do other stuff. It was all very weird, but as long as they didn't get too close to me while they were huffing and puffing and spraying sweat everywhere, that was fine with me. It will be interesting to see if social distancing becomes a permanent fixture. Part of me hopes so, because I'm not big on people getting too close. When you're on the telly, people often forget to respect your personal space. And in celebrity circles, you're constantly being hugged by strangers. I'll turn up somewhere and people I kind of know but not really will start chatting away to me like we're best mates. Maybe we'll all become like the Japanese and start bowing instead of shaking hands. That would suit me down to the ground.

Oh, and in case anyone was wondering, no, I didn't take up any hobbies during lockdown. Why would I? Just because I was suddenly in isolation that didn't mean there were suddenly loads of things I realised I wanted to do. Elsewhere, people were claiming they were learning to crochet, play a musical instrument or learn a new language. I'm 42. If I'd wanted to learn an instrument, I would have done it by now. And language-wise, English is serving me just fine. When I was playing cricket, a sports psychologist kept saying, 'Test yourself, do something outside your comfort zone. Maybe learn the piano?' I never took his advice. I know I could learn the piano, but I'm quite happy to sit there for hours doing nothing. Honestly, it's great, just switching off completely, like someone has taken the batteries out. I'll suddenly snap out of it, look at the clock and think, 'Wow, where did the day go? It's five o'clock already.'

Jigsaw puzzles seemed to be quite popular during lockdown. There were grown adults boasting about completing 500-piece puzzles on social media, as if they'd actually achieved some-thing. I was thinking, 'Of course you've completed it, you're a grown adult. It's not hard. You just have to be patient and find the pieces. It's not black magic. You start with the corners, then do the edges, then start filling the middle in.' And if they weren't doing puzzles, they were out jogging. The streets were filled with joggers, people who hadn't moved faster than a walk for years. Panting, spreading germs far and wide. It wasn't a pretty sight.

The one thing I did think about doing was writing some fiction. But I don't really like writing, which is a problem. I'm good with ideas, it's the putting it down on paper that's the issue. I can't type, so I'm a pen-and-paper man. Even if I have to write a longish email, I'll write it out with pen and paper, take a picture of it and send it as an attachment. People might think that's eccentric, but it makes perfect sense. Because I'm terrible at typing, it takes me so long to get words down that I lose my train of thought. But if I write with pen and paper, I can get my thoughts down quickly without forgetting anything.

The best part is the reaction you get from people, they're quite appreciative when they see a hand-written letter, even if it is on their computer screen. Who writes letters nowadays? But I don't think I'll be writing a novel anytime soon. As some wag said right at the start of lockdown, 'A lot of people are about to find out that the reason they haven't written a novel isn't because they haven't had time, it's because they don't have any talent.'

CHAPTER SEVEN

GUILTY PLEASURES

Like most people, I watched an awful lot of nonsense during lockdown. What else was there to do? Of course, I watched *Tiger King* on Netflix. Poor old Joe Exotic, he finally got what he wanted and achieved global fame and he's in prison for 20-odd years. He probably couldn't even watch it. There's a lesson in there somewhere, although Donald Trump will probably pardon him.

I actually thought Joe was all right, until it transpired that he drugged his lions and tigers and killed a load of them. Oh, and it didn't look great when one of his staff had their arm bitten off and all he was bothered about was losing a few quid (the maddest part about that episode was the fact that she didn't seem at all bothered). At the end of it, I came to the conclusion that Joe didn't even like big cats that much. As for his arch-nemesis Carole Baskin, she got away with something. I'm not sure what it was, but she's definitely a wrong 'un. But you know the really strange part about *Tiger King*? I thought it was going to be even more bonkers than it was, which may or may not be a reflection of where my head was at during the whole coronavirus madness.

One lockdown phenomenon that I didn't watch was the Michael Jordan documentary *The Last Dance*, because while Michael Jordan is obviously a legend, basketball is rubbish. I saw a game once in New York and left at half-time, despite having courtside tickets. You know what really annoyed me about it? The sound of the ball bouncing. I have an irrational hatred of balls bouncing. That might sound a bit weird coming from a former cricketer, but the ball doesn't really bounce in cricket. Well, it does, but you can't hear it. But if someone is bouncing a ball, whether it's the kids in the garden or a bunch of NBA players at Madison Square Garden, I can't handle it. It's up there with doors banging. Big things, fine. Small things can really set me off. I'll be sitting there thinking to myself, 'You really should let this go.' A few seconds later, I'll lose it.

Anyway, at this basketball game, it wasn't just the sound of the ball bouncing that was annoying, it was also the sound of trainers squeaking. And I couldn't understand why they didn't just put the ball in the hoop, without all the showing off. For all those reasons, the thought of watching a documentary about basketball filled me with dread. It didn't matter that everyone was banging on about it, I just couldn't bring myself to put it on. I think I'll watch and enjoy it once the hype has died down.

I'm told that a lot of the footage in *The Last Dance* was shot in the 1990s, long before reality TV took off. At least that meant that there was less playing up to the cameras than you see in fly-on-the-wall documentaries today. It was the same with the famous documentary of the 1997 British and Irish Lions tour of South Africa, *Living with Lions*. But it doesn't work any more, because the people in modern fly-on-the-wall documentaries know that they can become 'inadvertent' stars. For that reason, I can't even watch cricket documentaries, because they're not a true representation of a team. Plus, I always thought that the changing room was sacrosanct. When I was playing for England, the idea of inviting a camera crew in would sometimes crop up but I was always dead against it. I didn't even like having TV cameras in the changing room after we'd won a Test match, although my lads love *The Test*.

Gogglebox has gone the same way, in that the people on it now know that they can use it to launch a celebrity career. Saying that, I still love it and watched a lot of it during lockdown. One of my kids was a massive fan of it, they persuaded me to watch an episode and now I'm hooked. A few of them are scripted to within an inch of their lives, but there are some real belters on there, especially that grumpy Mancunian bloke with the dog. When I was in Australia recently, the first series of Aussie *Gogglebox* was just about to start and they just couldn't get their heads around it. They kept asking me to explain it to them, I'd tell them that it was people being filmed watching TV and talking about it, and they'd be completely dumbfounded.

What my Australian friends would have made of some of the TV ideas I've been pitched down the years is anyone's guess. What usually happens is I'll turn up at a meeting and someone will say, with a beaming smile on their face, 'You're really going to like this.' Someone else will start explaining what the programme idea is and after about 20 seconds I'll say, 'I'm going to have to stop you there. I don't like it at all.' One of the worst ideas pitched to me was 'celebrity rehab', which was like something Alan Partridge might have pitched to Tony Hayers, the fictional BBC director of programming. At first, I didn't know whether they wanted me to appear on the show or host it. And when they told me that they wanted me to host it, I said, 'Whoa, this is not for me. What is wrong with you?' They couldn't really understand why I thought it was a terrible idea, because these producers and TV execs are in a world of their own and always think that every idea they have is of major importance.

Mind you, I'm a bit of a hypocrite, because some programmes I watch are, by most people's moral standards, absolutely appalling. With *Naked Attraction*, the basic premise is this: there are six naked people hidden in booths and they gradually reveal themselves from the feet up. After each round, a fully-clothed chooser eliminates one of the naked people, until there are only two left, at which point the chooser also takes their clothes off before choosing who they want to go on a date with (presumably with their clothes on).

Then there are the programmes you watch that make you wonder if you're supposed to laugh or not. I watch *The Undateables*, which is a show about people with physical or learning disabilities trying to find a partner, and can't work out if its heart is in the right place or not. Every time I watch it, me and the same group of friends spend the whole episode texting each other, but it's difficult to know if I'm finding the right bits funny, or whether I'm supposed to find any of it funny. That's the same as a lot of things in life now, you'll see something or someone will say something and you'll find yourself suppressing the natural inclination to laugh. But I think I watch *The Undateables* from a good place, because I also find myself getting a bit choked up, especially when someone ends up falling in love on a date.

But it's amazing how some shows stay alive, because they are so near the knuckle, exploitative and just seem to cause problems all the time. Take *Love Island*. Four people connected to that show have taken their own lives, which should set alarm bells ringing. Feminist groups have raised concerns over the portrayal of women and their treatment by the blokes on the show, mental-health charities have attacked it for the negative impact it can have on viewers who are insecure about their bodies, and it's all just a bit tawdry. Personally, I think people should be allowed to watch whatever they want, and if that's what the contestants want to do, then let them crack on. But I do worry about the messages it sends out and what direction we're going in as a society.

I completely understand why programmes like *Strictly Come Dancing* and *MasterChef* get millions of viewers, because they're nice. Most people don't want to watch programmes that pit people against each other and try to appeal to their baser instincts, they want to watch programmes that are a bit fluffy and make them feel good about humanity. That's also why dramas like *Call the Midwife* and *Death in Paradise* get so many viewers, because they're mostly lovely and completely unremarkable and unchallenging, like televisual weed. No one is going to go to bed angry after watching either of those, even if so many people have died on that *Death in Paradise* island that the human population must be teetering on the brink of extinction.

I've seen the odd episode of *The Great British Bake Off*, which is about as fluffy as TV programming gets, but it's not what got me into baking. I've always been partial to making cakes, although the opportunities nowadays are few and far between. I'm not one of those people who feels the need to take photographs and share them with people, but I can also make a decent spaghetti Bolognese, chilli con carne or curry. I don't feel the need to make anything fancy at home, because I don't even eat anything fancy when I go out.

I've gone full circle. I started out with a very basic palate – what you might call a northern palate – before eating out at Heston Blumenthal's place and lots of other Michelin-starred restaurants when I started earning a few quid, where they bring out loads of little portions and you have to pretend everything is the best thing you've ever put in your mouth, and now I'd sooner have a takeaway curry, fish fingers with chips and beans or, if I do go out, a Toby Carvery. I find all that Michelin-starred food a bit ridiculous. Starters made to look like desserts, desserts made to look like savoury food, main courses that don't fill you up. I don't think anyone really likes that stuff as much as they say they do. Most of it is down to snobbery and fashion. Look at Greggs, one minute everyone was taking the piss out of them, now everyone's eating their food and saying how good it is. People really need to start thinking about things a bit more and go back to basics. It's cheaper and it's nicer.

I like Japanese food. To a point. It's fine. I don't dislike it. But mainly because I've been told it's healthy. But if I was on death row and the governor said to me, 'The chef can make you two things for your last meal: either a delicate sashimi salad or a massive battered cod with chips and mushy peas. What will it be?' you know what the answer's going to be. It's not really a choice, is it? That's the ultimate test of how much you really like a certain type of food, whether you'd consider it as a last meal. And let's be honest, you wouldn't even think of eating anything that you would find in Nobu. Who asks for sushi on death row? I bet it's never happened. I've read about the last meals they eat in America and it's all burgers and pizzas and massive tubs of ice cream. And never once a sorbet.

What even is sorbet? Who's it for? It's basically shit ice cream. Ice cream with all the fun removed. Don't get me started on sorbet. My favourite dessert is Viennetta. The noise when the knife breaks the exterior shell, magnificent. Like the start of a miniature avalanche in your bowl. I wasn't as big a fan of Ice Magic, that chocolate sauce that turned solid after you poured it on your ice cream. That was far too silly. And pointless. The whole point of chocolate sauce is that it looks all lovely and gooey. Why would you want it to go hard? It's then an inconvenient layer between the spoon and the ice cream, rather than adding to the loveliness. Ice Magic was trying to fix a problem that didn't exist, which is exactly what Peter Jones would say if someone tried to flog it on Dragons' Den today. Liquid chocolate is liquid chocolate, that's what makes it great. Why would you want it to cease being liquid chocolate once you'd squeezed it from the bottle? I don't understand some people, I really don't.

When it comes to ice cream itself, I'm very much a giant-tub-of-vanilla-ice-cream man, but only if it's on offer from the Co-op. I'm not paying £5.99 for a small tub of Ben & Jerry's cinnamon and gingerbread ice cream. Vanilla ice cream is a strange thing. When I was a kid, that's pretty much what ice cream was. That or chocolate or strawberry. Then it became a byword for boring, the flavour that was always chosen last in a Neapolitan. Now, everyone is trying to put a spin on it, to make it seem more interesting. Ice cream isn't just vanilla any more, it's Madagascan vanilla. No, no, no. I am not having that. I don't care where they got the vanilla from – Madagascar or Grimsby – or whether the ice cream has got little black dots in it, it's still just vanilla.

While we're on the subject, what the hell is gelato? I thought it was just Italian for ice cream until someone put me right. That's the thing about food, you can be eating it and thinking, 'Yeah, this is all right, but it's basically just ice cream', and someone will pop up and say, 'Actually, it's not the same as ice cream. It's better.' But if that person hadn't said anything, I would never have known. And because someone at some point decided gelato sounded a bit fancier than ice cream, that meant they could make it more expensive. Now when someone asks if I want a gelato, I'll get a bit snappy: 'No. I

don't. I just want a Mr Whippy. Preferably with a flake in it.'
Or a Magnum, which was an absolute game-changer when it
came along in the 1990s.

While the Mr Whippy was co-invented by Maggie Thatcher,
Roger Moore played a part in inventing the Magnum. Apparently, he happened to mention to someone at Wall's that his
one wish was for someone to invent a choc ice on a stick. Not an
end to famine and war, but a choc ice on a stick. And someone
did. The Magnum brought luxury to the world of sticked ice
creams, blew the Feast (which promised far more than it deliv-
ered), the Funny Foot (nice, but not actually very funny) and
the Fab (nowhere near substantial enough) out of the water.
I'd even dare to say that the Magnum rivalled the Cornetto for
supremacy in the ice-cream van's freezer.

But whether you ordered a Magnum or a Cornetto, the
ice-cream man knew you weren't messing about. You meant
business. When he saw you approaching his van, he knew
he wouldn't have to be scrambling around at the bottom of
his freezer for a Screwball, because you had graduated to
more sophisticated things. The Magnum and Cornetto were

aspirational, the ice-cream equivalents of an Audi Quattro and a Volkswagen Scirocco respectively.

The Cornetto has lots of different flavours, with the nutty one probably the king, but I reckon the Magnum trumped them all with its white chocolate version. Is white chocolate really chocolate? I don't care if it is or not, I love it. Dark chocolate, not so much. Everyone's eating the stuff nowadays, and they tell me it's more sophisticated than other kinds of chocolate, but I wouldn't let it pass my lips. It's for people who have allowed advertising people to convince them that it's somehow more healthy than milk chocolate. But they don't really enjoy eating it. They can't, because it's just so bitter. Like eating raw coffee beans. People might call me simple and unworldly, but I don't care.

I once put a tweet out about a great meal I had at a Toby Carvery in Macclesfield and people were having a go at me for being unsophisticated. But you can waste a lot of time pretending to like things you don't really like. As I got older, I started to realise that you've only got a certain amount of time left, so you want to spend time doing things you actually like, not what other people say you should like. I've been everywhere trying to find a better Sunday roast, but a Toby Carvery is honestly by far the best money can buy.

Toby Carvery does all the meats, all the veg, giant Yorkshire puddings, and you can pay £1.50 extra for an Alan Partridge big plate. I never get four meats (a turkey, beef and lamb medley is my thing, the white turkey meat offsetting the red beef and lamb, for health reasons, while gammon never even enters the equation) but just the fact you can blows my mind. Actually, I'm not being entirely honest, because I will usually double up on turkey, beef or lamb because of the lack of gammon. And when you get a big plate, they chuck in a couple of sausages, as well as an extra Yorkshire.

I don't know how they do it, but the turkey is never dry, like the stuff you get with a Christmas dinner. It's always the same on Christmas Day: someone will say, 'Lovely turkey, not too dry.' And I'll be thinking, 'But it is dry. You're just saying that to be nice. It's always dry. Every year.' But whenever you eat in a Toby Carvery, you just know someone is going to say at some point, 'This turkey's very moist. How do they do it?' And they won't be lying. They must have access to special turkeys. Maybe it's not turkey? Or they're supplied by mutant turkey breeders whose birds live in aircraft hangars. To be honest, I don't care what it is, it's beautiful. As for Toby's special gravy, that makes everything taste good. You could pour it on a lemon sorbet and it would improve it. I'd drink it straight from a mug. In fact, I have. It's the perfect restorative beverage on a cold winter's day.

In case anyone was wondering if I was angling for free food from Toby's, they already give it to me. When I put that aforementioned tweet out, they got in touch and offered me a Toby Carvery gold card, which entitles me to a hundred pounds' worth of roasts a month. That card is one of the best presents I've ever received, along with a Pizza Express card that I had for a while. Although I must admit, it's a bit tricky sometimes when you're well known and having free food thrown at you. When it gets to the embarrassing part when I have to pull out this card to get the free food, I take that opportunity to give the waiter a big chunk of what the bill would have been. That seems fair, and it means they look after us better than any waiter at the Ritz. Especially the lovely lad from the Bolton restaurant, who always turns a blind eye to an extra Yorkshire, and Liam from the Macclesfield branch, who knows a few people I know and pulls out all the stops. That man would slip me extra sausages until the cows came home.

I get a bit paranoid sometimes, because I think people in the queue behind me are thinking, 'Who the hell does he think he is? Just because he scored a few runs and took a few wickets for England once, he gets extra meat.' And they're probably getting a bit twitchy, because they're within touching distance of the food and they're probably thinking, 'Flintoff's gonna clean up here. I just know it. He's gonna snaffle those last two Yorkshires ...' Although I'm hearing on the street that queuing and helping yourself is a thing of the past since the pandemic. Apparently, you tell them what you want and they get it for you. That worries me: how do they know where to put things on your plate? And how do they know the correct ratio of one food item to the next? You can give them a rough guide, but you'd end up hating yourself: 'Sorry, no, a few more carrots. One less potato. Hmmm, that gravy has become a bit overwhelming ...'

Someone suggested I should bring a magic marker along and draw a diagram of where I want things to sit on the plate. That idea's got legs.

While we're on the subject of bringing your own stuff to restaurants, my mum and dad had a gathering at their house to celebrate my grandpa's eightieth birthday and I turned up with my own wine glass. My mum wasn't very impressed. She didn't say anything, but I could tell by the expression on her face: 'Who is this boy? I'm not sure I know him any more.' I never did it again.

Obviously, I don't drink any more, but I was always very particular when it came to glasses. If I was drinking Guinness, I'd have to drink it out of a Guinness glass. They have those grooves down the side to make gripping it easier. If I was drinking Peroni, it would have to be out of a Peroni glass. Stella, the same, even when they introduced the glass with a stem. Occasionally, the beverage–glass combination didn't work. I was never a fan of the San Miguel glass, always thought it tasted better in a basic pint pot. I recently discovered that even Corona have introduced their own glass. I reckon they thought, 'Jesus, this pandemic has given us a bad name, we're going to have to up our game. A segment of lime isn't going to get us through this.'

But back to Toby Carveries. I think people feel sorry for my wife, as if she's made to eat at Toby Carveries against her will. But we all love it. There's one between Bolton and Preston, so we meet my mum and dad there. I'm not sure it's as good as my mum's Sunday roast, but it's better than anything I could do, and why would I even bother trying?

Not only have I drunk gravy straight from a mug, I am also partial to a bowl of mushy peas, unaccompanied. Someone recently told me that the mushy peas they have in fish and chip shops aren't actually made of peas, but it makes no difference to me. They're wonderful, whatever they are. And they're a godsend for owners of fish and chip shops, because they don't make any money on fish any more because it's so expensive to buy. Next time you're in a chippy and you order mushy peas, keep a close eye on the owner's expression: he'll be beaming from ear to ear, I guarantee you, because it means he lives to fight another day.

I understand that fish and chip shops can be a bit of a mine-field for southerners visiting the north. There's the story of Peter Mandelson, former Labour MP for Hartlepool, pointing to mushy peas and asking for a helping of guacamole. Then there are scallops. People see the sign and think, '60p for a scallop? Very reasonable.' But when they're served up, they discover that fish-and-chip scallops are actually fat lumps of fried potato, and nothing to do with scallops that live in the sea.

There was also a documentary series called *The Game Changers* on Netflix, about the benefits of eating a plant-based diet, so a lot of people are into it now and it clearly works for some of them. But I just really like eating meat. And while I don't mind vegetables, I don't want them to be the main part of my meal. And vegans get on my nerves a little bit. Eat what you want, but don't tell me why you're eating it. I'm not inter-ested. People who don't eat meat are similar to non-drinkers. Chances are when you ask non-drinkers what they want to drink, they'll reply, 'Oh, I don't drink, I'll just have a sparkling water.' And chances are that when a vegan orders food, they'll say something along the lines of, 'I'm having the sun-dried tomato herb salad, because I'm a vegan.' That's their little way of letting you know that they're morally superior to you.

As I always say to my missus whenever she hints that maybe I should eat less meat, I could go on the internet and find hundreds of articles saying veganism isn't all it's cracked up to be. Whatever you want to believe in life, you'll find things to back up your arguments on the internet. That's why the internet as an experiment has backfired, because while it is a fount of all knowledge, a lot of that knowledge isn't factually correct.

CHAPTER EIGHT

THE END OF THE WORLD?

Obviously, climate change isn't a good thing, but I have a slightly more nuanced view of it than most people. Extinction Rebellion have a point, of course they do. But I'm not sure they go about things in entirely the right way. I realise we need to act to save the environment but pissing people off is not the way to go about it. Whenever Extinction Rebellion has a demonstration, it seems to backfire. There will be people closing airports with drones, stopping people getting to work or to hospital, gluing themselves to and climbing on roofs of trains (which are electric anyway) and when it's all over, members of the public who were previously sympathetic will be angry about their tactics.

What they don't seem to understand is that to achieve their aims they need the man on the street on their side. And when I say the man on the street, I mean anyone for whom environmental issues isn't the main preoccupation in their lives. By breaking laws and making the lives of ordinary working people a misery, they're just shooting themselves in the foot. Most people are trying to be more environmentally friendly in their own little way and want to get behind good causes. But they're not going to engage with anything more meaningful unless organisations like Extinction Rebellion come across as more sympathetic and a little less eccentric.

I think coronavirus showed how we should deal with climate change. People need to be told how to behave by their leaders, otherwise they just won't do what needs to be done. If governments were completely honest about what's going to happen if we don't take action – 'carry on as you are and you'll destroy the world by such and such a date, but do this, that and the other and you might just save it' – then most people would go along with it (although not everyone, especially in America, because some people don't like being told what to do).

On top of that – and this is where my views on climate change and the environment get a bit controversial – maybe this is just how humans are going to go out. It's a morbid, fatalistic view, I know, but maybe there are simply too many humans being born, not enough resources to go round and there's nothing we can do to stop us destroying the world. Maybe we're too far gone, too set in our ways to learn to do things differently. And anyway, we've had dinosaurs ruling the earth, we've had our go for a few hundred thousand years (which some people say is a short span of history, but to me sounds like quite a long time), so maybe it's time for another group to have a go, who are hopefully smarter than us. Maybe when the world ends, a super race will evolve who will make a better fist of things.

I should probably worry about things a little bit more than I do, but most of the time I just live in my own little bubble. It's not that I don't care about what's going on in the wider world, it's just that there are so many things to care about and so many responsibilities closer to home and not enough hours in the day. I worry about my kids growing up. I want them to be fit and healthy and achieve everything they want to achieve. I worry about them every time they leave the house, and I worry about how worried I'll be when they're a bit older, when they start going out in Manchester, which is only a few years down the line.

I also worry about worrying itself. It's great that people are becoming more and more aware of mental health. It's not great that it seems to be becoming more and more of a problem. People have always had mental illness, it's just that it used to be ignored. But there also seem to be more triggers nowadays. Social media causes a lot of anxiety and feelings of inadequacy among young people. Kids are constantly comparing themselves to their peers, which creates real pressure to be a certain way. Not necessarily to be perfect, but 'better' than they've been led to believe they are. I think previous generations were more content with their lot. Because life was less complicated and people simply had less stuff, they weren't always striving for 'better' things. It wasn't always about who's got the most or the fastest or the biggest.

The pressure on young people to look a certain way – i.e., perfect – is enormous now. You see teenage girls sculpted to within an inch of their lives. It wasn't that long ago that women in their thirties were walking around with grey hair, because hair dye didn't exist. But now if a female celebrity under the age of 50 has a grey hair – or hairy armpits or legs or eyebrows that are deemed to be too thick – it's some kind of scandal. The irony, of course, is that we now have young girls shaving their eyebrows off and drawing them back on, which just looks odd. And instead of having natural skin, they're orange. With jet-black hair.

But it's not just the girls. When I was a kid, no one went to the gym. It just wasn't a thing. Now, young lads are walking about with six packs. And they all wander about with their tops off. I'll be sat there thinking, 'Mate, that's ridiculous, put your top on!' Unless your washing machine is broken and you're trying to fix it, there's no reason to take your top off. I actually find it slightly offensive and it doesn't reflect well on a person. Either they're far too pleased with themselves or they're trying to compensate for something missing from their personality. Or both. And young lads nowadays shave everything. It's normal now for them to be like mannequins. Or dolphins.

I don't know when all this pubic gardening and body baldness started, but even I've got caught up in it. In fact, I've been Veeting for maybe 20 years. I just think it's wrong not to keep things neat and tidy down there. Not that I was a hairy person in the first place. I've never had to worry about my back, and my chest hair has never been unruly. But that's kind of the point: when did people start worrying about having back hair? Not only did it just used to be a thing that men had, it used to be seen as quite manly. Now, it's a problem.

It's mad when you think about it. For most of human history, it was just considered normal to have a pubic bush. Probably up until the twenty-first century. Now it's suddenly seen as slightly ridiculous. I'm told that internet porn changed the rules. It certainly wasn't *Razzle* or *Fiesta*. Whatever it was, it can't possibly be progress. Or maybe it is? Why would any woman want their man's cock and balls to look like a tramp smoking a cigarette? That's going to ruin an intimate moment. It's not like I'm going to post my old chap on Instagram, but I just see it as good manners to keep it all looking tidy. That said, people should be able to do what they want without ridicule. If you want to walk around with hairy armpits, do it. If you want hairy legs, good luck to you. Then again, I'm not sure I'd be that happy if my missus had hairy legs. But is that fair because I've never shaved mine (I had bald legs until I was about 17, so there's no way I'm getting rid of that). As you can probably tell, I'm very conflicted on this particular subject.

God knows what it must be like for kids who are overweight or too hairy or too this or too that or too whatever else. So many youth TV shows today are obsessed with how people look and not so much with the content of people's character. And it's having a real effect on men's mental health as well as women's. Eating disorders used to be seen as a female problem, but now one in four people with eating disorders are male. And because men find having an eating disorder so shameful, they're far less likely to ask for help.

I've had to take more notice of my appearance for practical reasons, because no one is going to hire a presenter who looks like he's just got out of bed. Shows have wardrobe budgets and the stylist on *A League of Their Own* has become a mate, so he's developed a sense of what I'll say yes or no to. He'll sometimes chuck in some wildcards – a shirt that's a bit tighter or more colourful than normal – and I'll at least try them on.

But it's a horrible feeling, standing there in front of a camera wearing something that's not really you. And as I've become more established, I've started to put my foot down a bit more. If someone hands me something that's going to make me look like Austin Powers, I'll just say to them, 'Absolutely not. Not a chance in hell.'

Having had a skinhead for so long while I was playing cricket, for the sake of convenience, I now have to spend quite a lot of time in the hairdresser's. If I'm filming *A League of Their Own*, my mate called Donald does my hair and make-up. If not, I go to a fella called Howard who lives down the road and I've known for about 20 years. I just don't really like meeting new people, I'm naturally suspicious. Whenever Jamie Redknapp introduces me to someone, he says, 'This is Freddie. He's a good lad, just doesn't like anyone. It took me eight years.' He's exaggerating, but I know what he means. I always start from a position of neutrality. The way I look at it, if you expect nothing, you won't be disappointed. If you end up liking someone, you'll be pleasantly surprised. And by not being one of those keenos who walks around pretending it's great to meet people all the time (which must be exhausting), you'll ensure that you don't end up with loads of acquaintances you don't really want to speak to. It's not a problem, you can't like everything and everyone. There's no shame in it.

The secret of happy haircuts is finding a hairdresser you can have comfortable silences with. And who can cut your hair properly. A few years ago, I was persuaded to try somewhere new, a bit posh-looking, with a hipster name like Hedge or Thatch or some such. But I knew I'd made a mistake as soon as I sat down because this fella immediately started chatting nine to the dozen. I thought, 'I've got to nip this in the bud, sharpish', shut my eyes and pretended to be asleep. It didn't work, because he carried on talking. So the only option I had left was to actually fall asleep. The last thing I remember him saying was something about the Man City striker Sergio Aguero, to which I replied, 'Yeah, I like him, he's a good player.' Then when I opened my eyes, he had a shaver in his hands. I said to him,

'Mate, what are you doing?'

'Putting a line in the side, like Aguero.'

'Mate, I said I like Aguero as a player, not that I wanted his haircut!'

Good job he didn't mention Bobby Charlton, I'd have walked out bald but for three strands of hair swept over the top of my head. As it was, I wore a cap for about a month because I looked like an absolute tit.

I don't know what I'd do if Donald or Howard disappeared, because going anywhere new makes me anxious. With Donald and Howard, I'm ready for them. Because I've known them so long, I know what to expect. With somewhere new, there's the whole feeling-out process: are they going to recognise me? Are they going to ask me what I do? Is everyone else in the hairdresser's going to start listening in on our conversation? Am I going to have to give them a begrudging tip when they've already charged me £30 just to trim the back and sides? I get embarrassed if I don't tip, feel guilty for some reason. But then I end up tipping even if someone has done a shit job. Or I tip waiting staff in restaurants if I have a good meal, even though they didn't cook it. And I get worried about the 10% service charge. Does the chef get that? Does the owner take it off him? Do I need to tip on top of that?

Back to appearances, it's not like I'm vain in everyday life. Well, maybe a little bit. But not that much. I wear the same clothes pretty much every day. I get up, slip into some leisurewear and go to the gym. And when I get home, I have a shower and put a tracksuit on. If I do go out, it takes me about 15 minutes to get ready. But I do think a lot more about my appearance now. I have to, because if I looked like I did when I was in my early twenties, I wouldn't get any work.

When I was playing cricket, I basically wore pyjamas every day. But it didn't matter what I looked like as long as I scored runs and took wickets. And the first time I had make-up done for TV, I couldn't get out of the chair quick enough. But now, I even have an opinion: 'Do I need a darker eye shadow? Would a beauty spot be too much?' Not really. I don't take myself that seriously. But I do care. Because you know what kind of people do my head in? Those who put a lot of effort into looking like shit. Putting effort in, when it came to appearances, used to mean turning up in a tuxedo, with shiny, Brylcreemed hair.

Now, it means spending time and money on looking like you've just got out of bed. I'll never be able to get my head around that.

CHAPTER NINE

SPORT TALK

Alas, lockdown wasn't all sitting around the house in my pants. Sometimes, it was sitting around in my house in my pants broadcasting to the nation.

talkSPORT had just had a bit of a shake-up, with Laura Woods taking over the breakfast show from Alan Brazil Monday to Wednesday, and they wanted to keep things light. Instead of chatting about newsy stuff, me, Laura and Ally McCoist mostly just had a bit of a laugh. I found that a bit weird at first, because I kept thinking we should have been mentioning coronavirus and the chaos it was causing, at least every now and again. But I soon realised that we were supposed to be a little chink in the clouds for four hours every morning. If people wanted grimness – lots of different people discussing the coronavirus casualty figures, the lack of PPE in hospitals, when the whole madness might finally come to an end – there were plenty of other channels doing that, including our sister station talkRADIO. We touched on it every now and again, because it would have been weird not to, but me spouting about very important things I didn't really know about wouldn't have been wise, it would have been downright dangerous.

It's strange how these opportunities arise. I'd done a bit of radio before, including a live show on BBC Radio 5 Live, which involved me interviewing various famous sportspeople (some of whom I'd never heard of), and enjoyed it. But there's no way I would have been able to do a breakfast radio show in normal times because of my other commitments and the idea of getting up at 3.30 a.m. and driving to a studio fills me with dread. You can make it sound good on paper, because the show finishes at 10 a.m. But I'd just be knackered for the rest of the day and not be able to do anything. And I'd be lying in bed every night, panicking about having to get up in a few hours and worrying about not getting enough sleep. But during lockdown, I was able to roll out of bed at 5.30 a.m., shuffle into my living room, turn on my laptop and I was ready to go. To be honest, had I not been on camera, I could have set my alarm for 5.55 and done it from my bed. I'm always trying to come up with projects that don't take me away from family (I haven't been successful at it so far) so it was perfect.

I made it quite clear to the people at talkSPORT that I wasn't a football aficionado, although I have started getting more into football recently, because of the kids. They watch anything: the Premier League, the Bundesliga, Serie A, La Liga. I'll watch *Match of the Day* and think, 'Where have I been all these years, this is amazing. And when did Alan Shearer stop being miserable and become so charming?'

I play a bit as well, with some mates over at Man City's indoor academy, and absolutely love it. I'm not Virgil van Dijk, but I can play to a half-decent standard. But I still don't really know what's going on. Luckily, my fellow centre-back is better than me, so I say to him, 'Do me a favour, tell me where to go and what to do and I'll be fine. Just don't leave me to my own devices, or we could be down five–nil by half-time.'

When I was a kid, I played a couple of games for Preston Boys and got scouted by Blackburn, I think. But I never turned up for the trial, because I knew I wasn't very good. I was just big, quite fast and someone who would get stuck in, which isn't enough to make it as a professional footballer. When I played cricket, I could read a game. I could see how everything was going to pan out, like when I was playing chess. But I had no football intelligence. I'd stand at the back and think, 'Where should I go? Who should I mark? What should I do if the ball comes to me?' It would baffle me; I wouldn't have a clue. So when Gary Lineker, Ian Wright and Shearer are breaking a game down, with all the graphics and arrows and what not, that's like magic to me.

On talkSPORT, Ally had the football covered anyway, and it was a chance to focus a bit more on other sports that don't always get a look in. Obviously, there wasn't much live sport to talk about, which made it a bit tricky at times. And while I spoke to the bosses about what they wanted from me, I didn't really get any guidance. There were periods when the only 'sport' was stories about furloughing. Hands up who knew that word before lockdown? Luckily, Laura, who has been presenting on Sky for years, is a consummate broadcaster and Ally is also brilliant and such a nice man. The best thing about Ally is that he is a great talker, to the extent that I was quite taken aback by it on my first day. As I soon worked out, it meant that it was my job to fill in the gaps. Saying we just winged it makes it sound unprofessional, but that's basically what we did: Laura played the passes, Ally ran with the ball and I tried to finish things off.

People ask me if it's terrifying, presenting a live radio show for four hours. It is a bit scary, but there are lots of adverts. After 13 minutes, I could pad downstairs in my slippers and get a brew. But it was more weird than scary, knowing that I was sitting on my own in my house and millions of people were listening. Instead of finding it stressful, it was more a case of being careful not to let my guard down, because I was sitting in my living room in my T-shirt. When I started doing it, I'd been living in a bubble for a few weeks, only really speaking to my family and close friends. So even having a conversation with Laura and Ally seemed bizarre. I could see them on my Zoom, but there was a slight delay and it made it more diffi-cult to read people, bounce off them and anticipate what was coming next. At times, it was almost like flying blind.

Before my first show, I made the mistake of going on Twitter. While most people were nice, there was a lot of negativity, mostly along the lines of, 'Fucking hell, what have talkSPORT got that dickhead Flintoff on for?' Jeez, people are ruthless on there. I found myself thinking, 'All right mate, it's only sport.' But to some people, sport is the most serious thing in the world, even during a global pandemic. If a nuclear bomb landed on London, you'd be able to hear voices coming from underneath the radioactive dust: 'This is bad and all that, but I hope this doesn't mean Spurs are going to delay sacking Mourinho ...'

I quickly worked out that presenting a sports show is very different to presenting an entertainment show, because everyone seems to have an opinion about sport, in the same way as everyone had an opinion on how to beat coronavirus, and some people get very angry if you've got a different opinion to them. Because I've never played professional football, some people thought I wasn't allowed to have an opinion on it, or indeed anything else. And even if I had the same opinion as them, they sometimes got upset because I didn't put the opinion across in the right way: 'Stop. Doing. Sport. Wrong!'

Most people knew it wasn't going to be perfect, given the unusual conditions. But others had absolutely no problem letting me know that they didn't like me, in a way that I've never experienced when presenting various TV shows. I suppose that made sense, because talkSPORT is essentially a station for football fans. Then there were the people upset that we weren't talking about sport enough. I couldn't get my head around that. There was genuinely no sport, we weren't making it up. Did they want us to pretend there was sport going on? I'm not going to lie to you, the strength of the criticism surprised me, I was getting called all sorts at 7.30 in the morning.

While I've never really got that tribal football-fan mentality, where people are absolutely vicious in their criticism, it did demonstrate how much people need sport in their lives and how upset they were to be without it. Sport is escapism, a release, gives people something to talk about and their lives meaning. Before lockdown, I would never have thought of myself as a sports fanatic, so I was surprised that I missed it so much. I just took it for granted that I could turn the TV on at any given moment and there would be some sport on, whether it was some cricket during the day, football on Wednesday evening or boxing on Saturday night. During lockdown, I'd find myself sticking the TV on, in the vain hope that some people somewhere on the planet were defying coronavirus and having a game of rugby or tennis. But, of course, there was nothing there, and I struggle watching old footage. It's not the same as watching the same film twice, because knowing the final score means that most of the drama is lost.

Lockdown even made me reassess the importance or otherwise of my sporting career, and I'm about to contradict myself completely (I'm allowed to do that, because it's my book). I'm often quite dismissive about my time as a cricketer, because it always struck me as a pointless trade that didn't really help anyone. But when sport suddenly disappeared, it made me realise that sport does affect people's lives, in that it makes people happy or sad or angry or frustrated or inspired. Maybe I did enhance people's lives a little bit. It's certainly true that I missed my kids playing sport, because I get so much satisfaction from watching them enjoy and do it well, whether it's football or cricket or anything else.

I guess lockdown proved the old adage that you only realise how much you love something when it's taken away. It also showed that it's okay to admit to missing unessential things, even during times of global crisis. I'm sure people missed lots of trivial things during the Second World War, even while other people were being killed all around them. That's just basic human nature.

About the only sport that soldiered on during lockdown was darts, although the players had to play a 'home tour' in their garages and former world champion Gary Anderson had to pull out because his WiFi signal wasn't strong enough. Let's be honest: Gary probably just couldn't be arsed, like most of the rest of us during lockdown.

Taking over from Alan Brazil, who had presented the show for the previous 20 years, was harder than taking over from Clarkson on *Top Gear*. I suppose some people just don't like change, but the figures suggested there were still plenty of people getting up at 6 a.m. to listen to it, so they can't have been that upset. And as far as I was concerned, at least it was getting me out of bed, breaking up the monotony and giving me a bit of routine, which I'd missed. When you're being told what to do all the time, like when I was playing cricket, you rebel a bit. But when it's gone, you realise how important it is.

When subjects came up that I wasn't bothered about, or guests were on who I didn't really know, it was a bit harder. Everyone was suddenly up in arms about what footballers got paid and I'd be thinking, 'Have they only just realised?' And sometimes I'd find myself discussing sportspeople I knew hardly anything about at 6.15, like when Arsenal's Mezut Özil refused to take a pay cut (apparently he gives a lot of money to charity – when you're a radio presenter, you quickly learn that some stories are a lot more complicated than you originally think).

As I've already mentioned, furloughing was a hot topic during lockdown. You had Premier League clubs mothballing non-playing staff and asking the government to pay some of their wages, which obviously didn't go down well with fans, because their players were still getting hundreds of thousands of pounds a week. Then you had county cricket clubs furloughing staff, which was a different situation entirely, because some of those clubs were right on the brink. Even Lancashire were struggling, not only because of the lack of cricket but also because of the lack of income from the hotel and conference room. As for the grassroots clubs, lots of them were in dire straits. And with the best will in the world, there's not much Lancashire could do for them. Me sending them a message of solidarity and singing 'Imagine' from my house in Altrincham wasn't really going to be much help, let's be honest.

Another lockdown staple turned out to be footballers ignoring government guidelines, like Aston Villa's Jack Grealish and Manchester City's Kyle Walker. Kyle allegedly had a party at his house. There couldn't have been much social distancing going on that night. I don't know what goes through people's heads. I mean, it's one thing having a couple of mates round for a few glasses of wine in your garden, another thing entirely filling your house up with ladies. But at least he gave us something to talk about for a few minutes. And to be honest, I felt more let down by joggers than footballers having sex parties. I was out one day with my missus and our new baby and these people kept running past, panting all over us and spraying us with sweat. I actually got quite angry about that. One of them ran straight through the middle of us, so I told him, in no uncertain terms, to behave himself. And when someone on a bike came too close, I stuck my arm out and let him have it as well. I wasn't too worried about us, but there was an old couple down the road who looked absolutely petrified. They were almost cowering, as if they'd spotted the Grim Reaper.

Then there was the story about the potential takeover of Newcastle by Saudi Arabia. I didn't know much about it, but I soon understood that Newcastle fans didn't like Mike Ashley, because he sells cheap sports gear but hasn't got enough money for their liking (even though they're quite happy to buy half-price trainers from his shops), but they seemed quite happy for their club to be owned by Saudi Arabia. Then you had the other fans who had been wanting him to sell the club for years but were having a go at him for selling to Saudi Arabia. Whatever the subject, I soon realised that once I'd taken a position on it, I had to remember what that was, because we'd keep coming back to the same story throughout the show. When you've only just woken up, four hours can seem like an eternity. But if my position had been different at the end of the show than it was at the start, that would have given the game away.

Because there were so many people struggling financially during lockdown, there was a lot of talk about the immorality of football. Should footballers be earning hundreds of thousands of pounds a week? Probably not. But if someone had offered to pay me two hundred grand a week to play cricket, I would have bitten their arm off. That's why it doesn't really make sense to give footballers grief. At least they're providing entertainment, unlike some people who work in the City, who are just moving money around and earning millions of pounds a year for doing it. And it's only immoral because society is structured in such a way that people who do important jobs don't earn anywhere near enough. That's not the fault of footballers, especially as plenty of them give a lot of their money away. And look at Manchester United's Marcus Rashford, who raised millions to provide free food for underprivileged kids and forced the government to change their policy.

One of the problems when it comes to talking about morals is that everyone's morals are different. Is what I earn for *A League of Their Own* or *Top Gear* immoral? (No, I'm not telling you how much I make.) Who decides? What is the cut-off point? The only way footballers' wages will come down is if people stop watching them play. But that's not happening, which presumably means hardly anyone objects on moral grounds. You could sell out Anfield and Old Trafford twice over for some games. But Premier League football isn't all fan-funded anyway, most of the big clubs are owned by ludicrously wealthy foreign businessmen. Manchester City are owned by an entire foreign state. So it wouldn't really matter to them if they had 40,000 people or one man and a dog watching their games. Fan boycotts would have more of an impact in the lower leagues, but those players don't earn as much anyway.

Of course, the morality of big money in sport isn't just a Premier League thing. I've seen stats that say cricket's Indian Premier League (IPL) is the richest competition in the world, in terms of what players earn per game. Someone like Virat Kohli is earning hundreds of thousands of pounds per game, while tens of millions of his countrymen are living in the kind of poverty most British people couldn't even imagine. But I played in the IPL and I don't remember my agent asking for less money because it all felt a bit immoral.

I actually think fans are more likely to turn their back on the Premier League because of the lack of competitiveness, rather than perceived immorality. Because the top five or six clubs have so much more money than everyone else, and the gap seems to be getting wider, it's all become very predictable. And if a competition is predictable, people are likely to stop watching, in the same way they'll stop watching a TV series that's been running for years and become repetitive. Americans understand that, which is why they have a draft system to at least try to give everyone a chance.

Yes, Liverpool won the title in 2020 for the first time in 30 years. But it was hardly a surprise, given how much money they spent on transfers and wages. And something's not right when only two or three teams are capable of winning the league at the start of the season (I know Leicester won it in 2015–16, but something like that will probably never happen again). If 17 or 18 teams in a 20-team league know they can't win it, it's difficult not to conclude that it's all a bit pointless. There was a time when the also-rans would maybe nick a cup here and there to keep the fans happy, but even that doesn't happen much anymore. Clubs like West Ham or Newcastle have absolutely zero chance of winning the Premier League and almost no chance of winning a cup. So if you're a fan, what have you got to look forward to each season? An outside chance of a seventh-place finish? Not getting relegated? It must be depressing. But people still go, week after week, year after year, knowing they've got no chance of doing anything. It's a strange phenomenon.

More and more, the Premier League resembles Formula 1. They're both incredibly slick products but they're not very exciting. Although I have an appreciation for Lewis Hamilton. And the really mad thing is that the Premier League is actually quite unpredictable compared to other European leagues. In Scotland, Celtic have won nine league titles in a row. No club apart from them and Rangers has won the league since 1985. In Italy, Juventus have also won nine in a row. In Germany, Bayern Munich have won eight in a row. In France, Paris

Saint-Germain have won seven of the last eight. In Spain, only two teams apart from Real Madrid and Barcelona have won the league in the twenty-first century. In Holland, only two teams apart from Ajax and PSV Eindhoven have won the league in the twenty-first century. It's all a bit daft.

I actually think it's a lot more enjoyable supporting a team in the lower leagues, because you never know what you're going to get from season to season. Your team might end up in relegation scrap, a promotion fight or be yo-yoing between the top and the bottom of the league all season. They might surprise you and go on a cup run. Supporting a sports team should be about experiencing the full range of emotions. Not sitting in the middle of the Premier League season after season, because you don't have quite as much money as the teams in the top six or seven. Or qualifying for Europe season after season, simply because your team is richer than most of the other teams.

Your team getting relegated might sting a bit, but at least it's character building. And when your team is battling to stay up all season and manages to avoid the drop on the final day, the elation is like winning the World Cup. On top of that, players are often fighting for their futures in the lower leagues, which adds another layer of jeopardy. If their team gets relegated, will they be offloaded? Will they end up at an even smaller club in an even lower league? Will they suddenly be on 50 per cent less money? Will they end up on the scrapheap? They're not as talented as the boys in the Premier League, but success and failure means every bit as much to them. Sure, watching Liverpool fizz the ball about and run rings around opponents is wonderful. But watching 22 players scrap for their lives in a League Two six-pointer has its own special appeal.

When I was a kid, I watched Preston quite a bit, when they were playing in the old Division Three. And recently, I started watching them again and have really enjoyed it. Don't get me wrong, I like watching Manchester City in the Premier League. They look after you so well, especially if you're in their Tunnel Club. That means getting to watch the players walk through a glass tunnel on their way to the pitch (which is a bit weird), eating beautiful food and watching the game from a big heated seat. But that's when the problem starts for me. Because the fans just expect their team to massacre the opposition, the atmosphere can be quite sterile when they're not.

Meanwhile, at Preston, you get a real sense of what it all means to the fans. They don't expect their team to win every week or to play well, but it's not about that. They desperately want them to succeed, but it's more about supporting them because it's their local team and the right thing to do. It's about the belonging and the community and the realisation that the team's success or failure will have a knock-on effect for the city as a whole, and I love it.

The tribal nature of football isn't always a good thing, but it can be. I feel the pride when I watch Preston. I desperately want them to do well and I can feel that everyone else does as well. I look around and see the same people sat in the same seats they've been sat in for years, through thick and mainly thin. You certainly won't find many Preston fans at Deepdale who aren't from the city. And while the quality isn't as good as it is at City, it's drama in the true sense, because you never know what's going to happen. Not long ago, I went to watch Preston at Deepdale and in the first half they played like Brazil. In the second half, they played like 11 blokes who had never seen a football before. God knows what the manager said to them at half-time, but it was one of the most bizarre transformations I've ever seen.

But even that's got to be more meaningful that watching City beating someone 5–0 and wondering why my heated seat isn't working. At the Etihad, I've seen people complain about their heated seat not being hot enough. When City were playing at Maine Road, before their move to the Etihad, a fan would buy a cup of Bovril if they were feeling a bit chilly. And I'll look around and see that some people aren't even watching. They'll be taking pictures of their food or themselves and presumably sticking them up on Instagram. In contrast, at another Preston game I went to there was a woman handing out ginger biscuits she'd baked. She took the lid off this Tupperware box and people were passing this box around. That's the nice side of tribalism in football. Mind you, she ran down the front and gobbed at the referee at half-time. Not really …

I don't know if sport ceases to be sport if it becomes predictable, but it certainly becomes more boring. The dictionary definition of sport includes the word 'compete', so the less competitive something is, the less it can claim to be sport. That's why international sport is often more compelling than club sport, because money is usually less of a deciding factor. One of the charms of watching England play sport, whether it's football, cricket or rugby union, is the unpredictability. In the last few years, we've seen the England football team get knocked out of the European Championships by Iceland and reach the semi-finals of the World Cup. One year, the England cricket team is beating Australia in the Ashes, the next they're losing to Holland in a World Cup. That makes being an England sports fan fun. And it mirrors my cricket career: on any given day I could score a load of runs, take a load of wickets or completely embarrass myself. And while English fans might grumble about their teams' failures, they secretly love it. We're not like Americans, who aren't interested in anything they're not good at. We like ups and downs, it reflects our national character and standing in the world. And we like having a moan.

With Laura in charge on talkSPORT, we were never short of things to discuss. And instead of constantly arguing about the latest VAR controversy, which is what most football chat seems to consist of nowadays, we were able to get to know guests properly. And when I wanted to mix things up a bit, I'd chuck in some conspiracy-theory chat. When that happened, suddenly everyone had an opinion and there were even newspaper headlines about me thinking the earth was shaped like a turnip and that Elvis was still alive. I'd seen a picture in one of the newspapers of a gardener at Graceland, who was the spit of Elvis, or as he might look now. But what people don't realise is that I'm saying this stuff for my own amusement. I don't really think Elvis is alive, I just said that I hoped he was alive. Just as I didn't really think the Loch Ness Monster might have come out of hiding during lockdown because of the lack of human activity. It was a joke!

Presenting a radio show like that is a real skill, because you can't really sit on the fence. If there's an argument going on about something that doesn't really interest me, I'll usually just stay out of it. I'm not the sort of person who says things for the sake of it, which makes me quite unusual nowadays, because everyone seems to think that you should have an opinion on everything, whether you know anything about it or not. If I didn't feel strongly about something, I'd try to relate it to something similar I'd been through during my career as a cricketer. That said, that's quite difficult to do when you're discussing footballers on three hundred grand a week potentially taking a pay cut, because it's not something I have any experience of. And if a subject came up that did interest me, I sometimes had to rein myself in a bit, because in the real world, away from the microphone, I don't always express myself in the most articulate way. And you can't really be effing and blinding on the radio at seven o'clock in the morning while people are eating their cereal.

I've always had a huge amount of respect for live broadcasters, people like Richard Bacon, who's presented shows on lots of different stations, and 5 Live's Nihal Arthanayake. And Alan Brazil is brilliant. The whole time he's been doing that show (he now does Thursdays and Fridays), he's never once sounded like he didn't want to be there. Like the best radio presenters, he seems interested in every word a guest says, can flit from subject to subject and comes across as knowledge-able about pretty much everything, which he can't possibly be. That's a real skill, natural or not. Ally McCoist is similar, in that he has that ability to natter away about anything, as if you're sitting in a pub with a pint. But he's been broadcasting for years now, what with *A Question of Sport* and his own chat show up in Scotland.

What I find with former sportspeople of an older vintage is that they just have so many great stories and tell them incred-ibly well. They don't talk a lot because they like the sound of their own voice, they just really enjoy entertaining people and making them laugh. That's why their stories get better every time they tell them. I'd even go as far as to say that older sportspeople are simply more interesting, probably because sport was more interesting when they were playing. Sport is so professional nowadays that youngsters don't really do much other than train and play, whereas the likes of Ally and Alan Brazil had a lot of fun away from the football pitch. Alan could write an entire book about horse racing, his love of wine and whatever else, while Ally even did a movie with Robert Duvall and Michael Keaton, called *A Shot at Glory*. It wasn't as if Ally just had a walk-on part, he was a headliner. I went on *A Question of Sport* when I was 20 and was in awe of him.

It's always weird when you see famous people pop up in places they're not 'supposed' to be. I was watching the Rocky film *Creed* in a cinema in Australia when the British boxer Tony Bellew suddenly appeared on the screen. I literally did a double take and wanted to shout, 'That's Tony Bellew! That's Tony Bellew!' Not that anyone in Australia would have known who Tony Bellew was, but I was just so excited.

As I'm sure Tony would tell you, when you become famous for one thing and start doing something completely different, the public sometimes find it difficult to deal with. They just struggle to compute it. Tony had this reputation as a mouthy, lairy boxer, but he's been on *A League of Their Own* a few times and is brilliant, probably the best guest we've ever had. He's game for a laugh, hams things up and is actually a bit of a softie under the hard exterior. But because he was a boxer, and people have certain preconceptions about boxers, I think he's struggling to carve out an identity for himself beyond the ring.

And if he does manage to, people will start to think he's two different people, just as they do with me.

There are honestly people out there who think Andrew Flintoff and Freddie Flintoff aren't the same person. But it doesn't bother me that people didn't know I played cricket. Let's face it, more people aren't into cricket than are. In fact, I'd say it's a good thing, because it suggests I've made a success of my second career. The same goes for someone like Alan Brazil, who was actually a very good footballer and played for Scotland in a World Cup, but lots of people know him only as a broadcaster. People not knowing he was an elite footballer is probably the best compliment he can receive. And Andrew Castle, the former tennis player, is a prime example of someone whose broadcasting career has been far more successful than his sporting one. But people aren't always accepting of ex-sportspeople trying to switch to another career. They'll see me pop up where I'm not 'supposed' to and think, 'Why is he on my TV?'

My mate Tom Davis was a scaffolder before he became a comedy writer and actor, and the comedian Romesh Ranganathan was a maths teacher. The fact they had 'normal' lives before becoming famous is seen as a good thing. But when an ex-sportsperson tries to have a crack at something else, people say, 'What the hell does he know? He should stick to cricket.' I had it with *Top Gear*: 'What does Flintoff know about cars?' But how does the fact that I once played cricket for a living have any influence on how well I can present a programme about cars? It makes no sense. People need to chill out a bit, instead of wanting people to stay in their box. In the 'real' world, people change careers all the time. And if ex-cricketer Imran Khan can be prime minister of Pakistan, then I can chat about a new car for a few minutes.

CHAPTER TEN

GETTING OLDER, GETTING BOLDER

There are certain tell-tale signs that you're getting old. When you find yourself seeking sanctuary in your own house, that's a big one. I know people who can sit in the toilet for half an hour at a time, scrolling through their phone. Like people would have done with a newspaper, before the internet ruined everything. That's never been me, I'm very much an in-and-out kind of guy, toilet-wise. But I understand the thinking. And maybe that will be me, eventually. If you've got four kids, you can lock yourself away under the stairs and get a bit of peace and quiet. Paradise, if you don't mind the smell of your own shit.

I have found myself sitting in the garage quite a bit. That's my haven. I've got my exercise bike in there, one of those Pelotons. Or sometimes I sit in a camp chair, stick some music on and just stare at the wall. Or I leave the door open and stare at my cars outside on the drive. I find it incredibly peaceful. Until I suddenly start thinking, 'What the hell have you become?' And then I'll have a bit of a panic and reply to myself, 'A tit. That's what you've become. An absolute tit.' But then I calm down again and think, 'Nothing wrong with getting old. It happens to everyone. Might as well embrace it.'

When you're younger, people think you're a bit odd if you want to sit on your own. If anyone under the age of 30 told their mates that they had a shed with its own power and they pottered around in there for fun, they'd get slaughtered. Everyone would be calling them an old man. But as you get older, you come to realise that spending time on your own is a necessity. Even if it's for only 20 minutes now and then. It's good to be an old man.

No one wants to be constantly surrounded by people. It's not natural. I'm sure cavemen chilled out on their own, sitting in a tree or on the edge of a lake, with their feet dangling in the water. The main attraction is the lack of noise. And it's amazing what you can achieve when you're on your own in a shed or a garage. You don't have to sit there with your headphones on. You can build a ship from matchsticks or sit under a blanket and write books, like Roald Dahl. Or, if you've got a greenhouse, you can grow vegetables. It doesn't even matter if the vegetables are rubbish and you don't bother eating them, it's the peace and contentment you get from nurturing them that counts.

The problem – and it's a very modern problem – is that sheds and garages aren't what they were. Not too long ago, a man sitting in a camp chair in his shed or garage would be surrounded by bags of compost and tins of paint. Now, they tend to be a bit more pimped up. People put gyms, giant speakers and DJ decks in there. So in reality, they're just swapping one kind of noise for a different kind of noise. That's why I like to keep my garage mainly low-tech. Apart from the Peloton, that doesn't make any noise anyway, I've got a rowing machine, some weights, a dartboard and a putting mat. But that doesn't even spit the ball back, I have to go and fetch it. I've got my bikes on the wall and a picture of me and Steve Harmison.

If I lived in Italy or Greece, I reckon I'd end up being one of those old blokes who sits out in the sun all day. I understand that completely. As it is, I'm not too far off jumping in the car, driving to the coast and staring at the sea for hours on end. I wouldn't even get out of the car, I'd just stare through the windscreen, probably while rain was lashing against it. I used to find people doing things like that a mystery, but I get it now. I'm not sure I like that I get it, but I do.

Let's face it, the future is my dad. He goes fishing. He never catches anything, but it's not about the fish, like growing vegetables isn't about the vegetables. He goes through all the rigmarole of setting everything up, and I assume he puts bait on his rod, but it's not really about that. There's just an understanding that when he says he's going fishing, that's code for, 'I just want some time on my own, and I will be gone for a set period of time.'

I can't see myself ever becoming a keen angler, but I've joined a golf club. In fact, I've joined two. But when it comes to golf, my biggest decision isn't which clubs I should waste my money on. It's, 'Should I get a normal push trolley or an electric one?' The thing is, the push trolley is fine for now. But maybe in five or six years, I'll need one with a bit of power, for the hills. As it is, I always hire a power caddy, one of those buggies that moves on its own. Like a golf Dalek. But I can never get it on the right setting, so that it matches the speed of my walk. I'm always either lagging slightly behind or it's trying to catch me up. If I was being paranoid, I'd think it didn't like me. Surely things haven't got that advanced, where power caddies are so intelligent they can throw strops?

During the pandemic, the golf clubs were closing a bit earlier than normal, which meant I couldn't hire a power caddy and had to get a push trolley instead. I'm not going to lie to you, that threw me. I was so disappointed about the lack of power caddy that I couldn't concentrate on my game. Over at Coombe Hill in Kingston, I couldn't even hire a push trolley, because of germs. When the man in the pro shop told me, I felt this wave of frustration rise inside me. All I could think was, 'My bag is bigger than Tiger Woods'. This is going to be the worst day of my life.'

But after a couple of holes, I had a little word with myself: 'Mate, who do you think you are? What have you become? Pull yourself together man. You've only just turned 40, you don't need a power caddy or a trolley. It's just a bag of clubs. And look around.

It's beautiful. Just crack on.' After that, I had a lovely round of golf with my mates, although I did buy a smaller bag from the shop. I find that the older you get, the more you crave comfort. You get complacent, so you have to keep checking yourself.

From a youngster's point of view, there are a lot of things that aren't great about getting older. But once you start getting older, you realise that embracing those things is preferable to pretending you're still young. Take clothes. Everyone experiments with different styles until they reach a certain age, when they settle on a look, either consciously or unconsciously. And that's pretty much them for the next 30 years, until they start wearing chunky cardigans and orthopaedic shoes.

I'm a tracksuit man. But I've got my own tracksuit style. I like to match it with a beanie hat and a gilet. I've got far too many gilets. I genuinely love them. I bought one, just to experiment, and now I've ended up with seven or eight, for every possible occasion. Big warm ones for winter. Lighter ones for those early spring days. Waterproof ones for the rain. And one of them is my favourite item of clothing. Not a Hugo Boss suit or a pair of Loake brogues, but a gilet.

I can't even explain why I like it so much. It's just so cosy. I'm not particularly proud of the fact. I mean, not so long ago, if someone had used the word 'gilet' in my presence, I would have laughed in their face. If I'd seen someone under the age of 40 wearing a gilet, I would have said, 'Look at this lad in a gilet. Who does he think he is?' The weird thing is, for years British people went around pretending they didn't know what a gilet was. Of course they did, it's just that they used to be called body warmers. But the fact is, I love gilets. They are magnificent items of clothing. Scratch what I said about not being proud of my love of gilets, I would gladly shout it from the rooftops.

There's no point raging against the dying of your youth, you've got to open your arms and say, 'Come and take me.' Otherwise you end up being one of those blokes in their forties and fifties, dressed like they're in their twenties, still slavishly following the latest trends, still hanging out in bars where everyone is half their age. I see those blokes on the school run, wearing baseball caps and skinny jeans with fat thighs and bellies pouring over the top of the belt. They'll also be wearing a tight designer T-shirt and a pair of Gucci trainers. I'll look at them and think, 'Mate, don't do it. Embrace comfort. At least embrace the gilet.'

I flirted with some of the stuff, so I know what I'm talking about. Especially when it comes to baseball caps. I looked like Steve Buscemi in that social media meme, except without the skateboard on his back: 'How do you do, fellow kids?' I had to have a little word with myself: 'Andrew, you've got children, have some dignity, stop wearing the baseball cap.'

I'm pretty certain I'm not having a midlife crisis. The fascination with fast cars would suggest different. But I've never really understood that accusation, because I would have loved driving fast cars when I was 17, it's just that I couldn't afford them. I think that's what happens when you get older, you end up buying the things you would have liked as a kid but didn't have the money to buy, whether it's Nike Air Jordans or cars. I don't think that's a midlife crisis necessarily, I think that's actually quite a nice thing.

My mate Dave has just bought himself a Ford Fiesta XR2, mark 1. In black. Not that I could drive it – I'm not sure I could get in it – but I totally understand why he's bought it, although he is bigger than me. Because when he was a kid, that's probably what he dreamt of driving. I know a lot of kids have posters of Lamborghinis or Ferraris on their walls, but they're just a fantasy. But when I was a kid, owning a Fiesta XR2 was a realistic ambition. Or something like a Sierra Cosworth or an Audi Quattro or an Austin Montego GTi, or a souped-up Ford Capri Ghia, like Del Boy drove in *Only Fools and Horse*, they were achievable.

Aside from nostalgia, the good thing about driving a car like a pimped-up Fiesta or Montego, rather than a Lamborghini or a Ferrari, is that you're not going to be paranoid about driving it. You reach an age when you start buying things and are afraid to use them, in case they get soiled or you feel like a tit. Like trainers. What are trainers for? To protect your foot and make doing sport more bearable. But when you get older, and start buying more expensive trainers, you don't want to put them on. It's like a mental block.

A few years ago, I was having a mooch around Sports Direct, which is like an Aladdin's cave to me (row upon row of hoodies and gilets) and I saw a pair of Travel Fox trainers.

This wave of nostalgia came over me, because I remembered being in Fleetwood with my auntie Joan, looking through the window of a sports shop and seeing a similar pair of Travel Foxes. Back then, they were about 70 quid, which was way too expensive. But now I could afford them, so I bought myself a pair. I was just so happy. But I've never worn them. I'm too old. I just love the fact I own a pair. I should add that on the same day I bought the Travel Foxes, I also bought five pairs of Dunlop Green Flash. They were only about £12 a pair. They were my back-up, the little run-arounds that do all the work while the flash cars sit idle under dust sheets in the garage.

I've started doing it with furniture as well, like my grand-parents. The footstool in my living room has a blanket on it, so it doesn't get dirty. But no one will ever see how nice it is, because of that blanket. It might as well be an upturned beer crate, like students use.

I'm the same with bikes. I've got one that I've cycled thou-sands of miles on. I've ridden that bike from Athens to London, all through Ireland and around Australia. It's not particularly expensive, just a Boardman, but I'm attached to it, in a way I've never been attached to a car. I love that bike. I've got another Boardman that's almost exactly the same, but I hardly use it, because it feels like I'm being unfaithful.

I've also got this other bike with deep-set wheels and electric gears. But I can't possibly ride it. How could I ride it? It's worth a fortune. Not that I paid for it, someone gave it to me. But that doesn't make any difference. What if it started raining and it got some mud on the wheels? Plus, I'd look a proper tit on it. A bike wanker. If you're going to ride a bike like that, you can't be overtaken going up hills. It can't happen, because it's so ludicrously expensive. And every time you heard someone coming up behind you, you'd be paranoid that they were on a 100-quid bike from Halfords. It would be like driving a Ferrari and being overtaken by a Vauxhall Corsa. It's so light, that's why they are so expensive. But it's a false economy – I don't want it made easier, I'm training and I'm 17 stone.

I must confess, I rode it once, during lockdown. I took a wrong turn and got punctures in both wheels. I opened my little saddle bag and there was nothing in there. I had all the Lycra gear on, which matched the bike, and everyone was stopping to ask if I needed any help. They were probably being lovely, but I couldn't help imagining they were sneering and laughing under their breath. In the end, I phoned up my mate Dave and asked him to come and help. When he arrived, he had an electric bike for me. So now I had to cycle home on this electric bike in all the gear. Electric bike folk are the scum of the roads. Normally, you get lots of nods and waves. On an electric bike, people look at you in complete disgust. I couldn't get home quick enough. I flicked it into the fastest gear and started flying past groups of cyclists. I'd give them a little greeting – 'Morning. Good day. Have a good ride' – and disappear into the distance. They were hating it. Absolutely hating it. After a while I thought, 'If you're hating me leaving you for dead, why don't you get one?!'

Since then, this ludicrously expensive bike with the deep-set tyres and electric gears hangs on the wall in the garage. When people see it, they always say, 'Oh, that's a nice bike.' And I immediately start talking about my Boardman, like a dad trying to divert attention to his hard-working kid who doesn't get enough attention.

I think a far bigger sign of a midlife crisis, cycling-wise, is the clothing. You get these people who wear all the branded stuff, as if they're a member of a Tour de France team. I don't get it. Why? You wouldn't stitch a load of fake sponsorship onto your golf polo shirt, to look like the pros. The big brand in cycling is Rapha. Don't get me wrong, they do some lovely gear. But some of their jerseys cost over a hundred quid. And unless you're Bradley Wiggins, you look like a complete whopper in it. Not least because everyone knows you've paid over a hundred quid for something you can get in Sports Direct for a tenner. You know when someone turns up in Rapha gear that they're more about the cafes than the cycling.

They're a strange bunch, cyclists. There's no getting away from it. Very tribal. Lots of them pretend to hate cars, even though they drive cars themselves. When it comes to the war between drivers and cyclists, I'm neutral. I can see why cyclists get upset with drivers, but I also think that cyclists do things to wind drivers up on purpose. Like riding two abreast and holding the traffic up. I know it's legal, but why not just ride in single file for a bit and let the traffic through? I was driving one day with the roof down and stopped at some traffic lights. This fella on a mountain bike came up on my inside and pulled over right in front of me. The traffic lights went green and he started huffing and puffing his way up this hill at about 1 mph, in the middle of the road. So I shouted at him, 'Sorry, mate, can you pull over, so I can get through?'

'I'm allowed to do this.'

'I know you are. But you're holding everyone up. Why not just pull over?'

'No.'

'Mate, I'm a cyclist myself. I know what you are and aren't allowed to do. But it's a case of being aware of other people.'

'The bike is the future. I can do what I want.'

'Yes, I know. But why would you want to be a knobhead?'

He couldn't answer that one.

But the whole driver–cyclist debate is a real minefield. For every knobhead like that fella, there are probably 10 knobhead drivers. It doesn't need to be a war. You get these drivers who shout at cyclists, 'Pay your road tax!' That doesn't even make sense, because everyone pays for the roads, whether they drive or not. Some of the rows are just daft, involving people who are just making stuff up as they go along, in order to bolster their position.

As wonderful as it is to be out on the open road on a bike, it can bloody hurt. The biggest pickle I ever got myself into was when I cycled from Athens to London. I hadn't been on a bike for years but I thought I could just jump on the saddle and get on with it. But after about three days, I couldn't feel my old fella. It just suddenly went numb, as if I'd trapped it in a door. It was like a dead fish. Obviously I couldn't just ignore it, that would have been very careless. So after another few days I said to the medic, 'Doc, I'm afraid you're going to have to have a look at my old fella, I can't feel it.' Luckily, I knew him from my time playing cricket for Lancashire. He took a look and was quite blasé: 'Oh, that's quite common in cyclists.' I was quite taken aback. I said to him, 'That's all well and good, doc, but does the feeling come back?' Apparently, it was to do with something called the penile nerve. The old fella only started to resurrect itself about three days after I arrived in London.

That felt like touch and go, not something I ever want to experience again. The weirdest thing was, because it was completely dead, it was almost like touching someone else's old fella. Each to their own, but that's not really something I've ever wanted to do. But I'm told women cyclists have it a lot worse. Apparently it's to do with the saddle, which is designed around the meat and two veg set-up, not a lady's parts. I think I'll leave it at that. Some of what I've been told is quite graphic.

I get self-conscious just walking about in the gear. Lycra doesn't leave a lot to the imagination. You order a coffee and the counter, where all the scones and flapjacks are laid out, is roughly old fella high. Sometimes I have to put my helmet over it, so that I achieve a double helmet. It's not like my old fella is particularly impressive, but I just feel like I'm exposing myself in front of women, children and dogs. Nobody needs to see that. I think there should be a rule that shorts have to be worn over the top. Almost like a reverse of the swimming pool rule in France, where they make you wear Speedos. Or that you have to wrap a towel around your midriff. Or maybe you shouldn't be allowed in shops at all? That might sound drastic, but it makes sense to me.

When I was a young man, if a mate started losing his hair, it was a gift. An open goal. All his mates would be in raptures: 'Are you finding it's taking you longer to wash your forehead? You should put your jam on your forehead and invite your hair down for tea.' That kind of stuff. But now I'm entering middle age, I feel a bit bad about that. People have feelings, and I've started having them as well. No one wants to lose their hair, whatever age you are. And people might laugh when you take the piss out of them, but they're probably hurting inside.

Nowadays, it's fairly normal for people to have hair transplants. So much so that I reckon bald men will be quite rare in a few generations' time. But hair transplants still sound like hell. Apparently, they take all the thick stuff from the back of your head and slap it on top (I think it's a bit more scientific than that. At least I hope so). And I assume that if they take it from the back of your head, they can take it from anywhere, like your arse. Although I wouldn't fancy that hairstyle. You'd end up looking like Art Garfunkel, except with even tighter curls. But that's just one process. I've seen another one where they put individual holes in your scalp and blood is pouring down your face. And if some men are prepared to go through that, that tells you how much they hate going bald and how wrong it is to take the piss out of them.

Cricketers led the way with hair transplants, we've been having them for decades now. Advanced Hair Studio led the way in the 1990s, which was when former Aussie spinner Greg Matthews became the first one to have a transplant. Graham Gooch liked the look of Greg's rug, followed suit, and soon everyone was getting involved: Darren Gough, Jacques Kallis, Shane Warne. I was on an England tour of Sri Lanka as a kid, having a few drinks in the bar, when Goochy's new hair fell off. The heat must have melted the glue. It just slipped down his forehead. I had to tell him and he fixed it in the bogs. The following day, some woman flew out from the London clinic to sort it out.

Mercifully, the technology has moved on since then. They don't just glue the thing on, like an old-fashioned rug. But the problem with it is, people get stuck with the same hairstyle for the next 20 years. And you get people saying that their hair is miraculously growing back, which is obviously not true. I think they become delusional. Talking of delusional, my old England teammate Anthony McGrath used to say that if a cow licked the top of your head, your hair would grow back. He'd say to people, 'Just hop over that fence, kneel in front of the cow and if it licks your head, hey presto, you'll have a thick mop of hair in no time. Trust me ...'

There was a time when people found hair transplants difficult to accept. Someone being bald one day and having a full head of hair the next was an affront to them. But I don't think people care about that anymore. And the likes of Goochy and Warney have played a big part in that, because they didn't try to hide it, they were shouting it from the rooftops. They might have got a bit of ribbing from their mates, but that probably only lasted a few weeks. If you can get new hair, and if it makes you feel better, why wouldn't you?

If I was getting it done, I'd want it to be pricey. If the bloke said it was going to cost 15 grand, I'd be asking why it didn't cost 30. Like if you were having a penis extension, you'd want it to cost a lot of money, so that you knew you were getting the very best treatment. Reassuringly expensive, like Stella Artois. You don't want to mess about with things like that, you want the best person on it. I'm a big haggler, always trying to get things for cheaper, whether it's a car, a house or a washing machine. But not in this case.

My brother went bald young, in his early twenties, and I felt for him. My dad's still got his hair, and he's in his seventies, so I don't know what went wrong with my brother. He used to dye it when he was a teenager, so that might have had something to do with it. The one good thing about going bald that young is that you don't really age for the next two decades. Thankfully, my hair is going absolutely nowhere. It's solid as a rock. I shaved it myself for about eight years, and I'm convinced that's what kept it thick. When you've got a shaved head, you don't use any hair products. No mousse, no gel, no clay, no putty. Just whatever shampoo is on offer at Boots. It means the top of your head is like an unsullied meadow, instead of a farmer's field, covered in pesticides (unlike what's underneath it, which is full of shit). It also kept the individual hairs on their toes. I reckon they were thinking, 'I will get back on his head, if it's the last thing I do. Push! Push!'

I look back at old photos of me with a shaved head and think, 'I wish someone had said to me, "Look at the state of it, grow it back!"' Actually, I do remember being on tour in New Zealand and sat on the back of the bus with my teammate Craig White, who had started losing his hair. He looked at me and said, 'Fred, can I ask you a question? You've got beautiful hair. Why do you shave it all off?' And I couldn't answer him. But I felt a bit guilty, because I hadn't realised how much hair meant to men who didn't have it.

One thing I do look back on with slight embarrassment is my bling phase. At one point, I thought I was 50 Cent. I had a diamond in my ear, for God's sake. And a big diamond wedding ring. I was dripping with bling. When I think about it now, it makes me shudder. I do still like to wear nice watches. I think that's quite a middle-aged thing. Not that

I've ever bought one, they've always been presents from my wife. Occasionally, I'll visit a watch shop knowing exactly what watch I want to buy. But I always back out. I just can't justify the expense. You can't get a Rolex for much less than five grand. You can buy a decent second-hand car for that. And I'm an anxious shopper anyway. I walk in a shop feeling fine and suddenly I don't want to be in there. I certainly don't see shopping as a leisure activity. You'll hear people talking about going shopping like it's a hobby, as if they're off for a round of golf. No. Not a chance. Shopping is not a hobby, it's a slightly stressful necessity.

One of the biggest giveaways that you're entering middle age is a sudden urge to live in the country, away from it all. When you're young, you like to be in the middle of everything. You think you're missing out if you're not. But you reach a certain age when you realise you're missing out on nothing, apart from noise, drunk people and bad bars. Don't get me wrong, I loved living in Manchester city centre when I was younger. I had a flat that was right in among it and had a ball. It wasn't great for my waistline and it probably ruined two or three years of my cricket career, but the freedom I had was amazing. I could drink into the early hours and order a pizza at 3am. What else does a man in his twenties want? You don't get many men in their twenties pining for the countryside.

Since then, I've sampled a bit of everything. After I retired, me and the missus moved to Dubai for a couple of years. We'd been on holiday there and enjoyed it. I think I was running away a little bit and I quickly saw it for what it was, which was a pretty weird place. Once you'd sat on the beach for a couple of afternoons and done some shopping, there wasn't much left to do. I spent a lot of time pining for England, I just missed home so much. And then we moved to Cobham in Surrey, which was lovely but a bit competitive for my liking. It was all about who had the most, the biggest, the best, the fastest. Although I was in a bad place at the time so it wasn't a fair reflection.

Now, we're back up north. At first, we went too country-side. That didn't work because we were still too young. We're now on the edge of a town in Cheshire, but I wouldn't mind moving back to the country. I'm hoping I can convince the family because that suits me. I don't really go out now, because I just want to be surrounded by my family and close friends. When you reach a certain age, you start thinking, 'Why am I standing in this bar surrounded by people I don't know when I could be sat at home with people I do?'

I love London but couldn't deal with living there. It's just so ridiculously busy all the time. At least it was before the pandemic. The Tube is one of the worst things in the world, especially during rush hour. Every time I get the Tube, I get off at the wrong stop. I find all those different lines so confusing. It's pressure I don't need in my life at my age. I also find the Tube quite intimidating. Everyone is just staring ahead of them, looking totally spaced out and angry. And London is maddeningly expensive. If I bought a flat down there, I'd spend the whole time really angry, wondering why I paid for two bedrooms in a concrete jungle when I could have got a five-bedroomed house with a big garden up north for the same money. Unless you absolutely have to live in London, it makes no sense.

If I had a magic wand, me, my family and close friends would all live in a little village in the countryside, that would be the perfect scenario. But, of course, I don't own a magic wand and life is never perfect. Not that everything about living in the countryside is great. I'd love a view, of rolling hills and water. That would be magnificent. But maybe only for a few weeks. In the summer. Winter, not so much. There's something very depressing about being in the middle of nowhere when driving rain is smashing against the windows. And if you lived by the sea, your cars would get damaged by the salt.

I find that I always want what I don't have. A lot of people are like that. When I lived in the country, I always wanted to go for a walk and seek out a coffee. Now I don't live in the country and have coffee shops just around the corner, I'd sooner put the kettle on and make a coffee myself. It's the same with the quietness of the countryside, which is great at first, something you'll keep commenting on: 'Oh, it's so lovely and peaceful out here.' But that quietness can become quite oppressive after a while and you start missing the sound of cars and human interaction. And if you did live in a village with all your mates, someone would end up pissing everyone else off. Guaranteed. We'd end up having a big row in the local pub and having to evict them.

Another good thing about living in the middle of nowhere is that you don't have to make any effort with your appearance. It's happening anyway. I'm basically turning into the late Steve Irwin, who seemed to wear the same clothes every day. I don't wear a beige shirt and shorts like Steve, but months slip past when I wear the same three pairs of jogging shorts and the same three black T-shirts. The only thing I switch up is my flat cap. I even started going out in tracksuits. Like Elton John.

There is a certain Cheshire look, sort of countryside chic. Lots of women in very expensive wellies and men in very expensive quilted jackets or jumpers hung over their shoulders. But you can bet your life those wellies, jackets or jumpers never get dirty. It's not like these people are farming folk. I've worn stuff like that in the past, when I was in my horseracing phase. I dressed like I thought a man who was into horses should dress – brown cords, wax jacket, flat cap – until I realised I probably wasn't really into horses but just liked going to the races and drinking Guinness in the fresh air. Or in the rain. When I first started dressing like that, my missus looked at me and said, 'I won't even bother saying anything, but you'll get bored with this eventually.' She knew. Like she always knows.

I don't worry about getting old, it just amazes me. I sometimes think, 'How am I in my forties? How have I got four kids? How is one of them six foot one with giant feet?' The worst part about getting old is the realisation that you'll never be able to do certain things again. It only recently dawned on me that I'll never play cricket again, and there will come a time when I can't do a lot of the physical things I'm able to do now. I get sore in the morning, I can't keep up with the kids when we go running.

I look at mates in their mid-forties and think, 'Jesus, they look old.' And then I'll look in the mirror and think, 'There's no getting away from it, you're starting to look old yourself.' I didn't think it would bother me, but it does a little bit. Every now and again, someone will post a picture of me online from a few years ago and I'll think, 'Who's this young fella?' And it will be me. The most frightening part about ageing is knowing that one morning you're going to look in the mirror and realise you've turned into your dad.

But while my appearance changing might bother me a little bit, actually getting old doesn't really. Obviously, I don't want to get ill, and that tends to happen the older you get. But I think that makes you look after yourself a little bit better. I want to go on for as long as possible, even make it to a hundred. As long as I'm relatively healthy and can do stuff, I wouldn't mind that at all. I just don't want to be a burden and sat there all day in an old people's home with a blanket over my legs, occasionally singing old songs, like anything by Stormzy.

What I don't understand about old people's homes is why the chairs are so uncomfortable. They're like the shitty chairs you get for visitors in hospitals, they don't even recline. If you were building an old people's home, you'd think that would be the most important thing, given that old people sit in them all day. It's got to be looked at, along with lots of stuff to do with old people. There's more and more old folk in this country, but they're still being ignored. The old model, where you just mothball old people in dreary homes, sit them in a circle and entertain them with Werther's Originals is not going to cut it with future generations. They won't put up with it. Instead of comfy chairs, they'll be demanding swimming pools and gyms and games consoles. And they should get it, instead of just a room with a window that they can stare out of, which costs them all the money they saved over the course of their working lives. It's shit the way old people are treated; we need to look after them better.

One of the strangest things about life is that we all know we're going to die but hardly anyone spends any time thinking about it. That's quite mind-blowing when you think about it. We go through life spending so much time making plans and trying to make some kind of sense of it all and we don't seem to care about the dying bit. You'd think old people would walk around with terrified looks on their faces, knowing that they were nearing the end, but most of them seem to be happier than young people. I suppose it's because no one knows what happens when you die and it's impossible to find out. Religious people think there's Heaven, but what happens after Heaven? Where do people go after that? There must be something else. Or do you get sent back down to earth again, for another crack at life? Maybe as a cockroach or a tree?

Until scientists can tell me otherwise, absolutely categorically, I'll not stop believing there's something else. I know they've got their Big Bang theory, but what was before the Big Bang? Exactly. They haven't thought about that. I think there's a chance we're not even here. We're pawns in a game that's being played, like in *The Matrix*. But then you have to ask yourself, whose game is it and who are they playing against? The questions never end. That's why we're programmed not to think about it, despite being so advanced. If we did, our brains would explode from the sheer mysteriousness of it all.

CHAPTER ELEVEN

CHRISTMAS CHEER

I must admit I'm a fan of Christmas. I love it. The carols, the Christmas pop songs when you're out doing your shopping. They remind me of a job I had one year, working in Woolworths, in charge of decorations. I even like Chris Rea's 'Driving Home' for Christmas. I'm not averse to listening to that one in July. But that's mainly because I've only got four albums on my phone: Christmas pop songs, that free one U2 sent out and I didn't know how to get rid of, Plan B's *The Defamation of Strickland Banks* and Neil Diamond's *Greatest Hits*. I must have listened to the Plan B album about 500 times, the same with Neil Diamond. Whenever I'm travelling, I have them on. But I've never listened to that U2 album. Does anyone know how to get rid of it?

My big problem with Christmas is presents, in that I don't like getting them. I find it a bit stressful, especially when someone gets me something extravagant. My kids get me personalised cards from Moonpig, which I will treasure for the rest of my life, because they put some effort into designing them. And I once got a coffee cup, which doesn't sound like much, but that's been in my car ever since. That said, if the kids ever become minted, they can buy me whatever they want.

I enjoy giving presents and seeing the happiness on people's faces. Not that there's always joy on people's faces, because I'm not a great buyer. I'm a panicker, I usually leave it to the last minute and hope I've pulled it out of the bag. But if someone doesn't like something I've bought them, it doesn't bother me. I keep the receipts, because it irritates me when people keep things they don't really want. I can see it on their faces, that pretend smile that's almost a grimace. And I'll think, 'I'm a big boy, you can tell me you don't like it and we'll go and get something else instead.' It's not like Santa's elves spent months knocking it up in their workshop, it was probably made in China by underpaid factory workers.

Give my wife her due, she gets me good things. Like my mum and dad when I was a kid, they never, ever got it wrong.

Not once. I'd come downstairs, walk in the back room and all the presents would be in there. Everyone would open them in front of each other and there would always be a big one for me and my brother. One year, my dad had been on strike for months but they somehow managed to get us an Amiga computer. I have no idea how they did it, although I do remember them eating a lot of egg and chips. Looking back, they must have gone without so much stuff themselves to be able to afford it.

Buying for women at Christmas is an absolute minefield, for the simple reason that women aren't men. How am I meant to know what a woman wants to wear? Lingerie is the biggest killer. Are you meant to buy what you want or what you think she'd like? I'll walk in the shop with the best intentions, get flustered and end up buying a pair of massive knickers, like Hattie Jacques wore in the *Carry On* films. I mean, how are you supposed to explain what your wife might want to the shop assistant? Or what shape her body is and how big certain things are? That's not something I really want to be discussing with a stranger in the middle of a shop. That's where the internet comes in handy. Or the Littlewoods catalogue. Saves on those awkward conversations.

If it's a particularly persistent shop assistant and you're shopping for lingerie, walking out is not easy. You can't exactly pretend you thought it was the electronics department: 'Where are your electric toothbrushes? This is the lingerie department, you say? Sorry, madam, I didn't realise. I thought they might be over there, by the girdles ...'

Kids won't believe you when you tell them, but there was a time, not so long ago, when the lingerie sections of clothing catalogues were an entry point for teenage boys, where they first laid eyes on semi-naked women. In the internet age, the entry point doesn't even bear thinking about. Let's just say it isn't a woman wearing a pair of sensible knickers in the Littlewoods catalogue, standing coyly with her back to the camera. You might say kids today are spoiled, in a very real sense. No wonder they never leave their bedrooms:

'I'm still playing Fortnite! Be down in a minute.'

'Yes, of course you are ...'

Who are they trying to kid?

As I've already said, I get nervous shopping for myself. If a shop assistant collars me as soon as I walk through the door, I immediately zone out and turn on my heels. I feel like I'm being watched, as if I'm in some Hitchcock psychological thriller. I'll convince myself that every time I pick an item of clothing up, they're hovering over my shoulder and mumbling, 'That's never going to fit him, the fat bastard. Who the hell does he think he is?' And if I do take a pile of clothes into the fitting room, I'll have to buy at least one item, otherwise the shop assistants will think I'm too fat to get into anything. I'll be standing there staring at one of those ludicrously bright mirrors they have in fitting rooms, wearing a pair of jeans that are two sizes too small for me, thinking, 'The brightest mirror does not lie. These jeans do not fit. But I will slim into them.' Two days later, I'll ask my missus to take them back.

Posh shops are the worst, a whole different level of stiff. When I used to take the kids with me when they were younger to posh shops, the assistants would be so stiff and watch us like hawks. You could tell they were on edge, getting ready to press the alarm under the desk and summon security. The northern accent didn't help. I'd feel like Fagin and his little gang of pick-pockets, let loose up the West End. If a posh shop assistant gave us a smile and left us to it, I'd repay them by ordering the kids to behave themselves. Otherwise, I'd whisper to them, 'Kids, consider this shop a playground, where anything goes.' With that, they'd start grabbing expensive sunglasses and trying them on, spraying each other with aftershave and perfume. And I'd watch the shop assistants getting flustered and think, 'No sympathy. Play the snobbery game with us and you will lose.'

Shop assistants in America are the busiest bastards. As soon as you set foot into a shop, they're all over you like flies on shit. If you can't find you what you came in for, they'll start suggesting alternatives: 'What about this? Or what about this? This would look great on you.' I'll be thinking, 'Erm, no, why would I take advice on what to wear from a complete stranger from America?' It used to really get on my nerves, until I learned that the reason American shop assistants are so busy isn't because they're just naturally lovely people, it's because they're all on commission. If too many people walk out of their shop without buying anything, they don't make much money.

Being a cricketer, I've been having random Christmases since my teenage years. I've experienced Christmases all over the world, from Australia to Pakistan to South Africa. I hated most of those Christmases, they were shocking. Yes, I got to party with my teammates, but only some of my teammates were actually mates. Some of them I didn't really like. And who wants to spend Christmas sitting around a table with random blokes and their families?

Nowadays, going out for dinner on Christmas Eve is a family tradition, while I prefer to spend Christmas Day at home. We all open our presents in the morning and the rest of the day is for eating. Apart from one year, when my missus went rogue and insisted the kids open some presents in the morning and some in the afternoon. I couldn't be doing with that. It doused the drama. Opening Christmas presents is all about the kids turning into animals for 15 minutes and leaving the entire room filled with wrapping paper and boxes so that it looks like a rubbish tip. Opening presents at different times of the day must be a southern thing, and I don't like it one bit.

After opening our presents, my mum and dad enter the fray. And then I do the meat: cook the turkey upside down, like Delia or Jamie or someone or other does it, and let all the juices flow into the breast. Keep spooning the fat all over it, before turning it over for the last half an hour. Remove the foil and hopefully you've nailed it. If you have nailed it, everyone will talk about it for the rest of the day, as if you're some kind of cookery genius who's performed some dark magic. Which is daft, because it's not like there's any magic to it. I'm not a turkey whisperer, I just put it in the oven and cook it upside down. And if you haven't nailed it, everyone will talk as if you've nailed it anyway. Those are some basic turkey rules.

But I have got it wrong, I must admit. I've underdone the turkey, in which case it ended up in a frying pan, and I've overdone the turkey, in which case there was nothing I could do to salvage the situation. I don't know a great deal about cookery, but I do know that you can't uncook a turkey.

Because I'm a fan of the Queen, we always sit round and watch her Christmas Message. I've got a lot of respect for her, but it's also a nostalgia thing. When I was a kid, my nan and grandpa would come round on Christmas Day and make sure we had it on the telly. My nan loved the Queen, even used to write letters to her. And she always got a reply. She'd write about her grandkids: 'Our Andrew's started playing for Lancashire and our Christopher's playing cricket as well.' Some of the letters she got back from the Queen were lovely. She also used to write to prime ministers. I remember her getting a reply from John Major, wishing me well in my career as a cricketer, because he's a massive cricket fan. A couple of years ago, I sat next to him at the Oval.

After the Queen's finished her message, I sit back and eat my own bodyweight in chocolate. I'm not into a lot of traditional Christmas foods, like Christmas pudding. I'd love to know the ratio of Christmas puddings sold to Christmas puddings eaten every year, it must be something like 100 to 1. I'm not a raisin or sultana man. I like the taste of them but the texture frightens me. And they're basically shrivelled, wizened, ill grapes. I can't get my head around that. You wouldn't eat anything else that was on its last legs. One time, my missus wanted to get me out of bed and threw a box of raisins at me. I played it cool, but it got to me, it really did. Raisins are like snakes to me. Even when my auntie Joan used to serve me up a buttered hot cross bun, I'd pick out the raisins and put them in my pockets. I didn't have the heart to tell her.

I have an aversion to mince pies for much the same reason. Who likes mince pies anyway? Anyone under 40? Not a chance would I eat one of those. The same with nuts. I like a pistachio but I can't be arsed taking them out of their shells. And I don't live in a Dickens novel, where a bowl of nuts was the stuff of a madman's dreams. I love a bowl of custard – I'll even eat it cold – but without the mince pie. But the idea of trifle fills me with dread. Trifle is the devil's work. Jelly, fruit, sponge, custard and sherry all mixed together? Whoever invented it must have been on acid. The sherry means I'm not allowed to eat it anyway. I can imagine being interviewed in a few years' time and the journalist saying, 'What got you back on the booze?' and me replying, 'My mum's trifle.'

My Christmas dessert of choice is a big slice of Victoria sponge. Not very Christmassy, you might think, but once you've got your cracker hat on, everything's Christmassy. That's the only thing about Christmas, there's a lot of feigned happiness. You'll pull a cracker, stick the hat on, show everyone the pair of nail clippers that's fallen out and everyone will act as if it's the best thing that's ever happened. And if a set of clockwork false teeth that can chatter and walk around the table falls out, it's as if Jesus has appeared.

The sizing for cracker hats is all over the place. Marks and Spencer need to hire a good milliner. One person's cracker hat will be sat on the top of their head at a jaunty angle, another person's will have slipped down their forehead so that it's covering their eyes, someone else's will be round their neck. I'll look around the table and think, 'What is happening here? Grandpa's 92 and he's got a cracker hat on. Have some dignity, man.' Meanwhile, he's telling me the turkey's nice and moist when he can barely chew it. Instead, he's letting it dissolve on his tongue, like a cough lozenge. Personally, I don't like wearing a cracker hat. I feel like standing up, slamming my hands on the table and screaming, 'I am not a paper king!' It's not even proper paper. It's old-school toilet paper. But I always bow to Christmas peer pressure. You just look like an old misery guts if you're not wearing one. And no one likes to be an old misery guts on Christmas Day – the family Scrooge – even if you are one.

When it comes to Christmas chocolates, I'm a Heroes rather than a Celebrations man. As far as I'm concerned, Cadbury win that one hands down. That said, each pick and mix has its pros and cons. I am a rare breed in that I love a miniature Bounty. In most houses, the Celebrations box is swimming with Bounties as Christmas Day draws to a close, but not in our house. I think it's because I like to suck my chocolate. That's why I'm a big fan of Yorkies, it's like sucking on miniature breeze blocks. But you pop a piece of Cadbury Caramel into your mouth and it's gone in seconds, and no one wants that.

Someone told me once that they play a Christmas Day game which involves Heroes versus Celebrations, in a Ryder Cup format. Heroes were the European team, Celebrations the US team, you'd have a blind draw and everyone would have to vote on the winner of each match. It was surprisingly tactical. Do Celebrations frontload their team with the big guns, like Mars and Snickers? Or do they chuck Bounty and Milky Way up front, as sacrificial lambs, having anticipated that Heroes would be leading out with Dairy Milk and Caramel, both titans of the chocolate world? Personally, I prefer charades. And I'm not sure it works, because everyone knows that Dairy Milk is king.

Once dinner is out of the way and the cracker hat has been shed and scraped into the bin with the leftover turkey, we'll all crash out and watch a Christmas film. And when it comes to family Christmas films, you can't beat *Elf* with Will Ferrell. And then I fall asleep. Actually, I'm usually asleep after about half an hour. And that's pretty much that for another year. I've never been a big fan of Boxing Day. When I was still on the booze, I'd wake up with a terrible hangover, because I'd been drinking since breakfast on Christmas Day, and still feeling stuffed. And then I'd have to run through a brick wall again. There'd be half a turkey that needed finishing, all the food that no one wanted to eat on Christmas Day and two crates of lager. I associate Boxing Day with groaning. People sprawled all over the house groaning. It's not the best day , but now I enjoy it as we go to my mums.

Of course, after Boxing Day is even worse. That awful void of pointlessness. The lost zone. No one knows what the date is, everyone keeps asking what day of the week it is. Mind you, the 27th was always a big day when we were kids, because it was my auntie's birthday and she'd have another party. But when she died, we lost the 27th as well. That just became another part of the lost zone. But we did gain the 28th recently, because that's when our last baby was born. Thinking about it, I might have another one and time it so that its arrival fills another gap between Boxing Day and new year. Just so we've got something to do. Rather than eating turkey and miniature Bounties.

As for New Year's Eve, it's the worst night of the year. By a country mile. You go out and wait for something great to happen that never happens. Even when I drank it was terrible. I don't need to be counting down to midnight, holding strangers' hands and dancing all over the place like an idiot. And when it got to midnight, nothing actually changed. It was just another day. It was all so forced, and there are few things worse in life than forced fun.

The only time it was half-decent was when I was a kid, when my auntie Pauline would have a party for all the family and I'd get to see my cousins. But as soon as that stopped, New Year's Eve turned to shit. Now, me and the missus never know what to do – because everyone thinks they have to do something – and end up doing nothing. And then you wake up the following morning and it's January. And as if January isn't bleak enough, some bright spark decided to make dry January a thing, although every month is dry for me. Why would anyone want to stop drinking in January? Surely it would be a better idea to say, 'What can we do to make January more fun?' Fun January. That makes a lot more sense to me.

CHAPTER TWELVE

THE FUTURE, OR MAKING IT UP AS WE GO ALONG

What will the future look like? It is a question that has exercised the minds of some of our greatest thinkers, from H.G. Wells to the person who made the Smash instant mashed potato adverts. But they usually get it wrong. For some reason, futurists are all obsessed with the same things, chief among them robot animals, flying cars and sustenance in the shape of pills. But how is anyone going to fit a Toby Carvery into a pill? Clearly, these people are not thinking deeply enough.

There's not a pill big enough for a Toby Carvery. How are you going to get all those meats and vegetables into a pill? It would have to be twice the size of a frisbee. And what would you do with the gravy? Try to incorporate it into the pill or pour it over the top before swallowing? It's the minor details these sci-fi writers often overlook.

I actually think our technology is far more advanced than we know. For example, I reckon they already have robots and computers that know what people are thinking without saying anything. But I think the tech companies and the authorities aren't letting us have it, because they know it would blow our minds and wouldn't necessarily be good for us. Because, let's face it, a lot of amazing technology isn't necessarily good for us. In case you hadn't noticed, the technological advance has slowed in recent years, in that there haven't been too many new developments. It's as if they've hit a brick wall. But they can't possibly have hit a brick wall, so there must be a backlog. There are all these mad patents piling up and at some point they're all going to be unleashed on us. And when that happens, who knows how society is going to react.

Sometimes the sci-fi folk get it right. George Orwell's *1984* seems to have got a lot of things right about politics and society. And *Back to the Future* came pretty close. In the second one, they nailed biometrics, virtual reality glasses, Bluetooth-style headsets and flatscreen TVs. But even they got flying cars wrong. Marty McFly was one of the great gilet wearers, 30 years ahead of his time, and you can also buy the self-lacing Nike trainers he wore in *Back to the Future II*. They cost about 30 grand. That's a lot of money, but if we have another lockdown and I get a bit bored, I can't rule out buying a pair.

Other futurists just make it up as they go along. Like Nostradamus. At the start of every year, some Nostradamus devotee will pop up and say, 'Nostradamus predicted there will be a great shock in the next 12 months.' No shit. Of course there's going to be a shock. Chances are, there will be quite a few of them. And every few years, people say Nostradamus predicted the world is about to end. And obviously it never happens. Not that Nostradamus gives a shit, he died about 500 years ago. You can't even hold him accountable for his nonsense.

I'm not sure about flying cars, they'd be too dangerous. It's all very well having a prang in a supermarket car park, but if you did that at 50 feet up, you could fall out of the sky and die. If flying cars ever do take off, I bet you there will be flying cyclists holding everyone up, just like before. I can picture them now, hovering about, cutting in front of the flying cars, getting angry about everything. And then they'll have to think of somewhere else for cars to go.

That's one of the reasons why it might become quite normal for people to go to space, because of traffic jams. I certainly wouldn't mind going up and having a look. Some people say it would be a bit dull, because there's nothing there. But that's ridiculous. Imagine staring down on your own planet. I can't even begin to imagine how incredible that would feel. You'd also be able to check that the world was actually round, and that governments hadn't been lying to us. And maybe you'd even bump into an alien life form. It's a long shot, but I'd say it's more likely to happen in space than Cheshire.

What would you say if an alien introduced himself? That's a big question. Chances are you'd have all these big ideas in your head, about how the universe had changed forever, but be so overwhelmed that you'd start blathering on about the most trivial things: 'All right? Nice to meet you. Erm, have you eaten? Do you even eat? I've got a Toby Carvery gold card if you fancy a trip to Macclesfield. Just say you're a friend of mine. The four meats will blow your mind. You don't get that on Pluto. But maybe give the gammon a swerve.'

Of course, aliens have already visited planet Earth. They made the pyramids. They must have, there's no other explanation. I know someone who studies Egyptology and even he thinks the only explanation is magic. And because we know that humans can't actually do magic, it must have been aliens. And they must have been all over the world, because there are pyramids all over the world: Africa, South America, the Antarctic. You can't move for pyramids. There's even one in Stockport. I don't think there are any tombs in that one, although there might be a few bodies under it.

Do you want to know something else about the pyramids? There is a bigger time gap between when the oldest Egyptian pyramids were built and the most recent pyramids were built than there is between the most recent pyramids being built and now. If that doesn't blow your mind, I don't know what will.

We live in a seriously weird and wonderful world, don't we?

INDEX

ACKNOWLEDGEMENTS

Thanks to David Luxton, Sara Drinkwater, Alita Butcher-Wallis, Katie Lydon, Matt Phillips, Beth Eynon, Ben Dirs, Tom Fordyce, Nikki Mander and all at Bonnier Books UK.

DO YOU KNOW WHAT?

Are there aliens out there somewhere?

What happens when I die?

What's the worst that can happen?

Do You Know What? is an unexpectedly helpful, occasionally silly and absorbing brain dump on life and everything it holds, from one of Britain's most-loved national treasures.

Out now

If you haven't yet read

DO YOU KNOW WHAT?

read on for a hilarious extract from Chapter One ...

CHAPTER 1

IN (ALMOST) TOO DEEP

Life beyond the comfort zone

I'm standing in a wrestling ring in a warehouse in Florida, surrounded by dozens of cameras, filming me from every conceivable angle. What looks like the entire cast of *Game of Thrones* are ringside, all wearing fluorescent Lycra. And all I can think is: 'I just want to get out of here.'

Before I know it, someone has shoved a microphone in my hand and shouted in my ear, 'Right, now your turn.' No going back now. Two minutes doesn't sound like much, but when you're so far out of your comfort zone you need satnav to find your way back, it feels like an eternity.

I launch into my routine, which I thought up during the walk to the ring: 'I'm from Preston, England, and I'm gonna hammer all of you and shake things up!'

It still makes me cringe just thinking about it. But as I'm climbing out of the ring, I think to myself, 'That was rubbish. I want another crack at it.'

I snatch the microphone back, climb back in and take in my surroundings for a few seconds. Everywhere I look there are weird and wonderful people, and I pick out a few obvious targets – a fella with a massive head, a fella with a big nose, a fella with a particularly bad haircut, a fella with a stupid voice – and let rip. The fella with a head like a melon gets it good and proper, big nose doesn't know what's hit him, the bloke with the man-bun looks like he might start crying. Two minutes go by and I can see the director trying to wind me up out of the corner of my eye, but I start shouting at him like a maniac, 'Oh no, I have not finished yet, just you try and stop me...' I'm like a man possessed. At this rate, wind-up man is going to have to wrench the microphone from my cold, dead hands.

My routine lasts ten minutes, and as I'm climbing out of the ring for the second time, all I can hear is absolute silence. Everyone else got a clap. I sit back down, feeling a bit self-conscious, and watch the room empty.

The acting coach comes over and says, 'That was good, well done.'

'Thanks, mate, but I don't think the others liked it much.'

'Don't worry about them. You can teach anyone to wrestle, but you've got to be able to get a reaction from the audience, whether good or bad. Wrestling fans hate vanilla. And one thing you weren't was vanilla.'

How did I end up in a wrestling ring in Tampa? It's a fair question – wrestling isn't a typical career progression for a former England cricketer. The simple answer is, I needed a job. I was living in Dubai at the time, drinking too much, eating anything I wanted, cruising through life. My day consisted of taking the kids to school at 7:30 – I'm not an early riser, so that was a nightmare, especially after a heavy night – before heading to the gym at the Burj Al Arab. The Burj is a six-star hotel, and ridiculous for it, because you don't have to do anything. You park your car and someone appears out of nowhere to take your keys. Someone carries your bag to the gym. You meet your bag at the gym and as you're getting undressed, a man is picking your clothes up to wash them. You get in the gym and as you're trying to put weights on the bar, someone steps in to do it for you. I'm surprised they don't offer to run for you as well.

After the gym, I'd sit on the beach for two or three hours. Every day I'd eat a fruit platter, because it was the cheapest thing on the menu, but it still cost about 30 quid. Then I'd go out and drink aimlessly in the evenings, and if I'd carried on like that I would have been skint. As it was, I was in a restaurant one night and both of my credit cards bounced. I looked around in a panic and saw the football manager Steve Bruce on another table. We had a mutual friend, so I went over and said, 'All right, Steve, nice to meet you. I'm a big fan, so and so says hello.' Then, after a while, I said, 'Look, Steve, bit of a problem, I can't pay my bill. Can you lend us a few quid?' That was my life in Dubai, but it wasn't really living.

In television, everyone is looking for a hook. So you've got to put yourself out there and throw ideas at people, and if it all starts sounding like that scene from *Alan Partridge*, when he's desperately pitching programme ideas to Tony Hayers, the fictional BBC commissioning editor – 'Arm-wrestling with Chas and Dave? Inner-city Sumo? Monkey tennis?' – that's all right, because someone will bite eventually if they think your idea has legs.

While I was sat on the beach, contemplating the fact that the grape I was eating probably cost £5 on its own, I thought about all the things that interested me, and settled on wrestling. When I was a kid, I'd watch WWE – WrestleMania, Royal Rumble – and even Big Daddy and Giant Haystacks of a Saturday afternoon on ITV. So I thought, 'Why not have a go?'

My original idea was to get trained up and fight The Undertaker at the Manchester Arena. I pitched my idea to my then management team, they thought it might work, we wrote up a treatment, presented it to Sky, and they loved it. Sky put me in touch with Vince McMahon, the boss of WWE, he gave it the thumbs-up and invited me over to train at the WWE's performance centre in Tampa, where American wrestling wannabes try out for a place in the big time. All of a sudden it was no longer a daydream: this mad idea I came up with on a beach in Dubai was actually going to happen.

To say I was a bit out of shape is an understatement. If I'm being completely honest, I'd completely let myself go. So I flew a trainer over to Dubai for six weeks (not a sentence I ever thought I'd write when I was a kid growing up on a council estate in Preston), got myself fit and bulked myself up, so that I thought I was massive. But no sooner had me and the missus arrived in Tampa, I thought that maybe this wasn't the place for us. We were sat there waiting for our bags to come off, next to this big American fella, and he let out this almighty fart. I said to the missus, 'Did you hear that?'

She replied, 'Yes, I did.'

He did it again, so I said to him, 'Mate, are you all right there?' and he looked at me like I was daft, as if lifting your leg and letting rip in the middle of an airport was the most natural thing in the world. Not for the first time on that trip, I thought to myself, 'These might not be my kind of people...'

The next morning, a car picks me up to take me to the wrestling school, and the missus decides she wants to come with me. We arrive at this unit, open the car door and this fella walks past who looks like he's come straight from the cantina in *Star Wars*. He's about six foot eight inches and 300 pounds of pure muscle, with a head on him the size of a basketball. This isn't a case of wondering if he's my kind of person, this is a case of wondering if he's a person at all.

My missus says to me, 'Are you sure you're all right with this?'

I reply, 'I'm fine, I'm fine.'

I'm not fine at all, I am absolutely shitting myself.